PASSION & PALATE

RECIPES FOR A GENEROUS TABLE

JOHN HOWIE

PHOTOGRAPHY: ANGIE NORWOOD BROWNE

FOOD STYLIST: PATTY WITTMANN

Enjoy!
Chef
John Howie

SHINSHINCHEZ LLC

First edition 2011

Printed in Canada

Author: John Howie

Photographer: Angie Norwood Browne

Food Stylist: Patty Wittmann

Narrative Copy: Kathryn Gilmore

Copy Editor: Judy Gouldthorpe

Project Management: Jody Ericson Dorow

Design: Nancy Gellos

Publisher: ShinShinChez LLC

ISBN-978-0-9827225-1-0

ShinShinChez LLC

2212 Queen Anne Avenue North #334

Seattle, WA 98109

www.shinshinchez.com

TABLE OF CONTENTS

FOREWORD

ATTENTION THAT WANDERS in the kitchen may result in a burned crust or a separated sauce; cooking is, after all, a tricky combination of chemistry and taste, a gastronomic mixture of science and art. Within the pages of this book, you will become acquainted with John Howie, whose unwavering focus on the culinary details of the professional kitchen has inspired truly tasty results. His attention in the kitchen has delighted the palates of the frequent guests to his many successful restaurants. In my close association with John over the years, I have been privileged to observe his ability to balance business with pleasure. I have seen the pride he has in his family, witnessed his enjoyment of the company of friends, and experienced his devotion to the surrounding community. One moment he may be negotiating prices with a product distributor, and the next, hurrying off to his son's baseball practice. He can recall every small financial detail along with the number of times his Duke Blue Devil basketball team has been in the Final Four, and conveniently forgets how many times my Michigan State Spartans have. On Thanksgiving, he will arrange food and service for more than a hundred local homeless families while attending to the financial travel needs of one of his chefs. John has the unusual ability to combine a generous personal style with a business acumen that completes a recipe for success. What is his secret? One could argue that he is a great multi-tasker or perhaps it's just his personality type. I think it's his immense respect and appreciation for both his personal life and his business life — he realizes that one is better with the other. John's secret is his attention to detail and his ability to combine chemistry, taste, science and art, and balance that with love. I feel confident that these pages will give you the opportunity to become acquainted with John and share in some of his culinary creations that have made him such an important force within the Seattle restaurant community, as well as some insight into John's heart.

ERIK LIEDHOLM
PARTNER
COMPANY WINE DIRECTOR - ADVANCED SOMMELIER
JOHN HOWIE RESTAURANT GROUP

PREFACE

I HAVE FOND MEMORIES of my early childhood, many of which revolve around food. The incredible summer corn feeds shared with neighbors and family in my birth state of Illinois. The amazing salmon BBQs after fishing at Westport, Washington. The sweet baby clams and juicy oysters we would harvest and shuck during our visits to Hood Canal. My mom's chocolate mayonnaise cake, which I demanded for every birthday. My grandma's black-eyed peas, smoky BBQ, and tomato and cucumber sandwiches back in Charlotte, North Carolina. My stepfather's rich smoked salmon and fresh cooked Dungeness crab. Food has always had my attention.

My mother, although never a gourmet cook, was a great cook, as evidenced by some of her recipes that grace the book. I believe that between them, she and my grandmother Grace Howie built the foundation of my passion and my palate for great food. From simple fresh foods to amazing ethnic dishes, the development of my palate came in large part from the great home cooking of the ladies in my life during my early years.

As for my passion, I believe there are many factors that drive people to become who they are. Some are good and some difficult, but that is what life is all about and what it brings to each of us. We can choose to accept it and grow from it or let it crush us. I chose the former. I believe that my path of determination and drive was set long before I was even born. You see, it's in my DNA.

Although my father's life was short, he still had a tremendous influence on my life. Like my father, I have never been one to let my free time go by freely.

Although my childhood was not exactly normal and support systems at times were lacking, I will always love my mother and must give her credit for my eventual success. She had a difficult life, from being shipped to a children's home where she was abused to the early death of the love of her life (my father). She always loved and cared for her children. I'm sure that in large part, my ambition and drive can be attributed to my mom. She was a strong woman, and when life threw her curve balls, she always took a big swing. She worked hard to raise three children the best she could — not perfect but the effort was always there. She influenced my palate with her great cooking, and my passion with her drive to take care of her children. She will always be loved.

People always ask me how I have the energy to run more than one restaurant, coach my kid's sports teams, and participate in so many charitable events. Where do I find the time? To these questions I must answer that I love staying busy — it's my nature.

I've been thinking about writing this cookbook for the past seven years. There are several reasons why I wanted to publish this book. From having a vehicle that provides our guests' favorite recipes for them, to giving my guests, friends and family some insight into what molds me to be who I am. And the obvious — it's great promotion for the restaurants, and we might make a little money.

The cookbook recipe-testing process has been an eye-opening experience for all of us. Many of our recipe testers can't believe the steps and the levels it takes to produce some of their restaurant favorites. Some of these recipe testers were intimidated at first, but throughout the process came to understand that the complexity of the recipes is what brings the complexity to the final dish. The most common comments were "Now I know why we like your restaurant so much!" and "It seemed like so much to do, but in the end it was worth it!" Not to say that all of the recipes in the book are complicated. I have my share of simple tasty recipes, too. Throughout the process, I found much of the feedback incredibly helpful, so much so that I even went back and made changes to the recipes to better them for the home cook.

But I didn't want this cookbook to be just another recipe book. I wanted it to be as much about my journey and the people who have taken that journey with me as it was about the food. To gain greater insight into that journey, my publishers and cowriters interviewed my family, my friends, my partners and our guests.

What we have now is more than a recipe book — it's a chronicle of a journey to achieve a vision that is so much more than the successful restaurant business.

I have been blessed. God has poured out his blessings on me, and my family, although my life has not always been easy. If we didn't go through the difficult times, we would never appreciate the good times. But many people have not been so lucky, and the majority of their lives have been one challenge after another. These are the people I want to help, the ones to whom I want to provide resources and positive motivation, so they will be encouraged to go out and do the same someday.

Along the way, I hope that I have set an example for others. At the printing of this book we have over 350 employees in our company, the majority of whom have participated in or given their money to one or more of our charitable events. I find our people who are committed to helping others a source of great pride. I'm grateful and blessed to have such an amazing group to work with.

When I opened Seastar Restaurant & Raw Bar on March 11, 2002, it was my goal to be a positive influence in the community, to "Never Say NO!" to any charitable organization. A lofty goal to say the least, but one that up until now we have worked hard to achieve.

I have never been hungry. Okay, that's not true; if I had never been hungry, I would likely never have eaten my way to this incredibly cuddly physique. A better way to put it is: I have never been without the ability to satisfy my hunger. I can't even imagine how awful that would be — especially for a parent watching a child suffer from hunger. That is why I have always been involved with organizations working to eliminate hunger.

I must admit I have a soft spot in my heart for children — to see a child suffer in any way torments me. This subject hits very close to home. My younger son, JoJo, was diagnosed with a mild form of muscular dystrophy at an early age. Luckily he has found that a strong exercise program is a great way to combat his illness, and it has kept it in check most of his life. In this I am also blessed.

I have high hopes for my book. I hope that this book encourages you to challenge your culinary skills. That you find a recipe or several that become family favorites and bring joy to your home. I hope that it will fire you up for whatever you're passionate about, that you find my story inspiring and it calls you to act on that inspiration.

INTRODUCTION

I REMEMBER THE DAY like it was yesterday. Me and my son JoJo — hanging out together at Mariners Stadium. Jojo was seven at the time. It was a rare sunny day back in 2001. The M's were winning. I had my favorite stadium meal — a steaming hot barbecued beef sandwich — perched on my lap. Stan Javier came up to bat. I knew Stan could hit, but I was pretty invested in my sandwich so I didn't think twice about my glove, carefully stowed away under my seat amongst discarded sunflower seed shells. And then — crack. He slugged it. Line drive home run. And the ball came screaming toward us. In a flash, I had to decide between holding on to my huge plate of food or tossing it aside and grabbing for my mitt. But I did neither. Like a lunatic, I stood up and shoved my bare hand up in front of my son as the ball hurtled toward us. Then the guy in front of us reached up and bumped my hand, the ball ricocheted off the heel of my now-sore hand . . . I watched as the ball bounced away . . . back onto the field where it came from. I was crushed. But not because I didn't get the ball. It was the words JoJo spoke just after the fielder tossed the ball to someone else in the stands. "Dad!" he yelled. "You dropped my dream!"

Those words have haunted me ever since. The thought of disappointing my son is unbearable. And today, when I reflect on that afternoon at the ballpark, it makes me think about my own dreams. And I can tell you this. When I was my son's age, I would never have dreamed I'd have the life I have today. I certainly never dreamed I would be a chef.

I was born in Chicago in 1960. My mom, Elsie Marie Douglas, was a stewardess. She had, at one time, won the crown for Miss Crawford County and was the first runner-up for Miss Pennsylvania. My father, John Harvey Howie Jr., was a very driven man. After graduating from Duke University, he enlisted in the Air Force, where he became a pilot and served our great country as a B-52 bomber pilot in the Korean War. After returning home he continued his flight career with United Airlines. Believe it or not, even his career with United had a culinary influence on me. One of the best memories I have is that when my father returned from a flight, he would bring home small packets of nuts, macadamia nuts, yes, real macadamia nuts. My palate was spoiled at an early age.

For the first four years of my life, we were a middle-class American family living in Chicago and Denver. My father's job as a pilot for United Airlines allowed him a lot of downtime. He used his downtime to work as a real estate agent, and as one of the first urban farmers, well maybe suburban — we leased a couple of acres of farmland directly behind the real estate office. We grew corn, tomatoes, cucumbers and pumpkins, and he would stay in the fields until dusk, often coming home bearing armfuls of his harvest. This was my first exposure to farming and was a huge influence on my wanting to promote the use of local farmers for our restaurants.

My father was also a generous man. One day he loaded his VW bug with pumpkins to bring to the kids in the neighborhood. It was October 10, 1964 — 12 days before my fourth birthday. I was supposed to be with him. To this day I can't remember why I wasn't. But Dad never made it home. A woman driving a massive wood-paneled station wagon T-boned his VW Beetle into a telephone pole. He died at the scene.

I don't remember much about that day. I've heard that my mom, upon hearing, crumbled to the ground. What I do remember is the next morning. I couldn't wake Mom up no matter how loud I yelled or how hard I shook her. So I went into the kitchen and grabbed some pots and pans and jumped up and down on her bed, banging them as loudly as I could. But she was so heavily medicated she didn't budge. Mom was never the same after my father died. She married my stepfather, Phil Bagwill, who brought us to Seattle. But the marriage was short-lived. She was a hardworking woman and did the best she could, taking care of me and my sisters. But the drinking began at some point, and many nights she returned home late in the evening, usually intoxicated. I think turning to a bottle of vodka helped her to forget the past and deaden her pain.

Throughout my youth, Mom expected a lot of me. She came to depend on me to take care of things. From the age of 10, I would come home from school to clean the house and cook dinner for my sisters. My first memories of being in the kitchen revolve around mixing together packages of cheap ground beef and Hamburger Helper and tearing apart a head of iceberg lettuce. Not exactly gourmet cuisine. To this day, I still have an unnatural affection for Catalina dressing.

There are some fond memories. I remember standing next to Mom as she stirred huge pots of tomato sauce riddled with caramelized onions. And I can recall digging into my favorite meals of green pepper beef and homemade lasagna oozing with cheese. Food quickly became a source of solace in our household, and for a time at least, when Mom cooked, everyone enjoyed her cooking and she seemed happy.

From the age of 11 until I was 15, I was the man of the house. I think what saved me from abandoning my responsibilities and running away was the work ethic that was instilled in me from an early age. I was my father's son. I had an irrepressible urge to keep busy. But while I was a responsible young kid, I was also my mother's son. I turned to drinking and carousing early on, often coming home to feed my sisters only to leave after dinner and then stay out all night. If I wanted to take money from my mom's wallet, I helped myself. Despite the fact that I never failed to take care of my sisters, I felt the lure of independence and took advantage of my freedom. Whenever I could, I would escape, using whatever I could to forget about my life.

This sense of independence came to a stop when Mom's drinking escalated. One day I was holding the garage door open for her and she passed out behind the wheel of her car, nearly running me over. This was a wakeup call — she finally started to acknowledge the depth of her problems. And she tried to quit. But she was on her own and it didn't work. Ultimately, she was hospitalized, and one of my sisters and I were placed in foster care. While it was only a six-week stint, my time in the home was a low point. My most vivid memory is of a fight with another kid that ended with a dirty pitchfork being thrust into my foot. He hit an artery, and to this day I can remember the blood pulsing out of my work boot.

After six weeks I moved back in with Mom. I can only imagine how difficult it must have been for her to come to terms with the fact that her children had been placed in foster care. As a child, she too had been forced out of her home to live with strangers. The stories she told described it as a time of fear and sadness. She didn't have it easy growing up. And I know it weighed on her — her inability to care for her children. She tried to make it work after she got sober. She attempted to play the role of mother, telling me what to do, how to behave. But I wanted nothing to do with it. I had already tasted freedom and there was no turning back. So at the age of 15, I got a job and started to earn my own money. And I left home soon thereafter.

I moved around a bit at first, living with friends in small, underfurnished apartments. I stayed in school until my senior year of high school, but found that a structured school environment just wasn't for me. I took my GED and started at Bellevue Community College. That didn't last long, as I was more interested in partying and hanging out with my friends. And to support this independent lifestyle, I needed to work. It was merely chance that my first job was in a restaurant. It was the only place that would hire me. Early on I bused tables and made $1.05 an hour, plus tips. That first job lasted three months, ending abruptly when the health department shut the restaurant down.

Being a cocky young kid, I applied for a pantry chef position at Emmett's, a fine dining restaurant and, at the time, *the* place to be. I had no cooking experience, just the time I had spent clearing tables of dirty dishes at a restaurant that was closed because of health violations. But the sous chef who interviewed me decided to take a chance on me. He hired me as a pantry cook, and I spent my days in school and my nights making salads and cold appetizers and watching the whirlwind of activity around me. Never one to shy away from hard work, I thrived in the frenzied environment of the busy kitchen.

Within six months I was running the line on Sunday and Monday nights. Granted, we only had 25 to 30 covers, but this was pretty sophisticated and elegant fare, especially for a 16-year-old rookie. I picked it up quickly. I was a born perfectionist, so in my mind I wanted to believe that every plate I put out was pristine. And I happily found that the time I had spent with my mother in the kitchen early on had left a lasting impression. Soon after starting at Emmett's, I realized I had an appreciation and passion for good food. Mostly because I loved to eat. I found that I could taste a dish and have a very good idea of how to re-create it. Even better, I found that what was pleasing to my palate was pleasing to others.

My time at Emmett's opened my eyes. I learned to appreciate fresh ingredients and exacting cutting techniques. I was learning my craft. I was falling in love with cooking. And there was nothing in the world like the immediate gratification I received from hearing the praise of a satisfied guest or my own stomach.

Despite the fact that I felt at home in the kitchen, I still didn't know that I wanted to do this for the rest of my life. It was just a job. I got fired after about nine months. I don't recall the exact reason, but I'm sure I deserved it. Being a smug teenager, I figured I'd find another job without a problem. I didn't figure, however, that nobody would believe I had worked on and even run the line at one of the top restaurants in town at the age of 16. People who interviewed me called me a liar. Nothing I could say would persuade anyone to hire me as a cook.

So I had to start at the bottom, a step I originally had passed by. I took a job as a dishwasher at a steak house chain and started to work my way up again. They served 500 to 600 dinners every night and I got to clean every plate. I walked out at the end of every night wet and wrinkled from head to toe. But I spent my time watching the kitchen. Trying to learn whatever I could about how a restaurant worked. After a short time I was promoted to fry cook. I only stayed about four months. My time was short there because despite the fact that I needed that job, I couldn't take it. My time at Emmett's, where the emphasis was on fresh ingredients and beautifully designed dishes that awed the guests, had spoiled me. I could not come to terms with the mechanical way in which this industrial-size kitchen served their guests. Cooking off hundreds of steaks every afternoon and rewarming them every night worked for them. It just didn't work for me. I wanted to serve quality meals cooked to order, not precooked and warmed up.

During my time off I would cook for my friends, and I came to like the praise they lavished on me. I wasn't cooking up anything particularly special — just good solid food, fettuccine Alfredo and steak bordelaise. And my friends inevitably asked for more. I realized that what I liked to eat was what others liked to eat, and this would be the basis of my future menus and creations.

So I kept at it, landing a sauté cook position at The Butcher, another well-known restaurant in town. And this is when things started to click. The chef recognized my abilities and gave me an increasing amount of responsibility and creative license. After a time I also worked weekends alone in the kitchen as the prep lead. But I think the fast pace of the sauté cook position was my favorite.

The owner would call every so often in the middle of dinner service, telling us to keep the restaurant open late that night because the Seattle SuperSonics would be coming by. The Sonics were on fire at the time, one of the top basketball teams in the country. And being a huge sports fan, I was thrilled to be in their midst, serving up huge charred steaks and the ever-popular batter-dipped Monte Cristo sandwiches. This was the time when I saw my culinary skills improving, and my confidence grew. I was becoming a chef.

I never trained professionally. I was never instructed on how to hold a knife, how to properly poach an egg, how to debone a duck. I learned by watching and mimicking. I appreciated early on the importance of precision. There is a reason that today my own line cooks are given a ruler and measuring spoons on their first day in my kitchens. I know that a ⅛-inch dice of onion has a vastly different flavor profile than a ¼-inch dice, and I want my cooks to understand that, too. Not to mention the visual appeal of symmetrical cuts. And for me, this attention to detail is the difference between a good dish and a great one — one that can be re-created time and again.

One of the most rewarding parts of my job is teaching others in my kitchens how to become better chefs. Working with them to discover new flavor profiles. Looking on with satisfaction as they put out plate after plate of perfectly flawless food. Watching their culinary and people skills grow. It's almost as gratifying to see the personal growth of my people as it is to see the satisfied look on a guest's face as they take that first bite.

I learned a lot about food at every place I worked — and I worked at a lot of places. After hobnobbing with the Sonics I moved from restaurant to restaurant, sometimes two at a time, taking on increasing responsibilities and growing my culinary knowledge and skills. During the 1980s, I worked at a number of restaurants, including 13 Coins and Boondock's, Sundecker's & Greenthumbs. At one point I held three jobs at once, one of which was in a restaurant named Sunday's, located in an old church where diners sat under four-story-high stained glass windows while the town's hottest disco vibrated down in the basement. Then I learned how to cook Creole and Cajun food at Simon's Restaurant & Piano Bar — blackened catfish, étouffée, jambalaya, gumbo. Not that they served much of the Cajun creations, but my chef, Kim Hales, was trained at Commander's Palace, and I took full advantage of his knowledge. Besides, this was food that I loved to eat. And flavors that still influence my menus to this day.

As I approached my fourth year at Simon's Restaurant, I started getting calls. I guess word got out that I was putting out some pretty good food. That I was a hard worker who was able to manage a kitchen crew. When the call came from Restaurants Unlimited, Inc., a Seattle-based restaurant company, I initially put them off. I was happy where I was, being groomed for the top chef position in our hot new restaurant being built downtown. But they persisted and I finally agreed to join them — making what would ultimately be the best move in my career to date.

When I started in the restaurant business, it was all about the food. I loved to eat and learned quickly that I also had a passion and a palate for being creative. At one point I finally realized that I wanted to be a chef, so in the early years I focused almost exclusively on perfecting my craft. But when I began with Restaurants Unlimited, I started to learn the management side of the business.

Oddly enough, I found that I might be as passionate about numbers and people as I was about food. I wore a lot of hats at various Restaurants Unlimited properties, and it was during this time that I really got to build my business skills. When I first joined Restaurants Unlimited, they called their chefs and sous-chefs kitchen managers and assistant kitchen managers. Food decisions were made centrally on a corporate level. I recommended that each chef be given more freedom to be creative — to display their own personality and put out food with a local touch. This allowed each individual restaurant to establish an identity and, ultimately, put out food that was much more pleasing to their clientele. Now I was bringing to them a culinary expertise and a desire to have that infiltrate the entire restaurant company. Within six months they agreed to have chefs and sous-chefs, not kitchen managers and assistant kitchen managers. One of the things I enjoyed most about working at RUI was how they listened to their people. I was motivated to make positive change for the company, and I had a lot of ideas.

I took on the general manager's responsibilities when my GM at Triples was asked to assume other responsibilities and suddenly became unavailable. We had a weekly reporting system, so I had to learn what was involved with a P & L statement, how to manage the restaurant's labor costs, and how to manage people better. I trained and was taught specific management styles and philosophies, many of which were foreign to me, but I liked what I was learning and put it to work. I was taken through my first personality profile, which helps you better understand who you are and what you can do to best work with others. I came out off the charts dominate/direct, no surprise. It gave me some clear directives on what I needed to do to become a better manager of people and helped me understand how I needed to work with other personalities. I worked on myself for a couple of years and came back to retake the test. To my surprise the results looked exactly the same. I wondered how could this be, thinking, I have worked on this, I know I am different, I know I have changed. And then they told me, "No, you are not different. You have just learned how to get better results from the people you work with. But you are still who you are."

One day all the chefs who worked for various Restaurants Unlimited properties were taken on a boat cruise around Puget Sound with founder Rich Komen. As we drifted by a newly built marina, he pointed out a spot on the water where his new restaurant would be built. He talked about it in glowing terms. I knew then that I was going to be the chef of that new restaurant — not because I was offered the job, but because I was determined to be the chef of that new restaurant. I felt a great amount of pride when I was chosen as the executive chef of Palisade. In large part I felt it showed that Rich Komen had a lot of trust in who I was and what I could bring to the project. I was challenged and I was excited to help him build his dream restaurant.

The experiences I had at Restaurants Unlimited built my own restaurant philosophy, and Rich Komen was a huge influence on me. He would say, "The guests will tell you what they want. Take care of your guests and the money will take care of itself." Restaurants Unlimited took a very raw chef and made him a restaurateur by simply teaching him management philosophy skills and the financial side of the business. For this I will always be appreciative and grateful to have spent 14 years of my life at RUI.

When I opened Seastar in 2002, my vision was "To be the Pacific Northwest's premier seafood restaurant." We put that message out there because we knew that if you are going to have a goal like that, you'd better state it and you'd better go after it, or you'll never get it. I also knew that I needed the right people, and the people I chose to work with were people I trusted and had worked with for years. And I knew they had the same goal that I had, that they were more concerned about taking care of the guests than they were about their bottom line or our bottom line. Many of them took pay cuts to come work with me, knowing that in the long run, it would pay off for them. They wanted to be a part of what we were going to accomplish together and what we were going after, and knew that if they put in the time, the effort and kept that guest-first attitude, we would succeed.

And I have always believed that if I don't take care of my employees, I can't take care of my guests. Having a core group of people who came with me allowed me to be more selective about who we were going to add to the staff. We had 95 positions to fill, and we had 1,500 applicants interested in those jobs. There were written questions, several interviews and background checks. I personally met with 150 applicants for what we called their third and final interview. I would ask people how they would create an environment of hospitality, and I would listen carefully to what they thought hospitality was and how they would create it. I would talk about having very diverse groups of people and how we need to have respect for the individual and for the job class. How every job is important. I talked about how it was essential to create this environment of respect and how we were looking to each and every crew member to make this a better place to work. We were going through this process to ensure we were hiring the right people, people who would make Seastar the best place to work. And last but not least, we were opening a fine dining restaurant and they needed to understand that they couldn't just be order takers, they couldn't just look at this as their own personal ATM, but they had to come in here on a day-to-day basis with a plan on how they were going to be better at their jobs. That's the kind of people I look for. I expect a lot. And my expectation is that everyone comes to work with an attitude of respect — for the food, their coworkers, and our guests.

Chefs are known to be perfectionists, especially when it comes to food. And I am definitely guilty of this. For whatever reason, my penchant for perfectionism has spread to all aspects of my restaurants. I know that this attention to detail — whether it's noticing a chip on a serving platter and pulling it off the table before we open or cleaning a scuff off a wall — drives a lot of people crazy. But I can't help it. I can't sit idle watching someone do a job that is merely adequate when I know they can do better. So I am constantly mentoring. Some would call it nitpicking. Or worse. But today I have people working alongside me who have been with me for over 20 years. I believe this is because we all take great pride in what we do. We all push each other to excel.

It took me years to develop this management style. Early on in my career, I struggled with delegating. I remember vividly what I call the "crème brûlée incident." It was during my first month as chef of Scott's Bar & Grill. My pantry cook came to me every morning to ask how many crème brûlées we needed. And I would tell her. Every morning. Finally Craig, my general manager, said to me, "You know, you're never going to grow anybody if you keep telling them what to do all the time." And then he quizzed me about how I determined ordering amounts, and when I explained, he asked if my pantry cook was capable of figuring it out herself. So the next day, she asked me the same question and I turned it around. Then I taught her how to figure it out on a daily basis. And I never got another question about crème brûlée. This was my first real management success — I saw the light and knew that I would use that same skill again and again throughout my management career.

Being a good manager is like being a good parent. There is care and love that come with this, as much as there is ownership. Like a good parent, you set clear, concise expectations for the people you are working with so they have a good understanding of what it is they have to do, believe they can do it, and are willing to do it. Then you make sure they do the work that needs to be done, to the level they have agreed to. Then you either praise them for doing it well or hold them accountable for changing their behavior so they do it right the next time.

Today I am able to truly let go. I have chefs I trust to run my kitchens without a second thought. And managers who control the bottom line as if they were running their own restaurants. Primarily because they are. All of the managers and chefs at my restaurants are partners both figuratively and practically. They are my family, my friends and my business partners. I have established a culture of accountability that has raised the level of excellence of the entire staff, of the entire company, and has allowed me to let go of the minutiae. This is the main reason why I have successful restaurants.

I know this sounds simple. But depending on others was not my natural MO. I was a self-reliant man who thought I knew everything, and I had little room for trust in my life. But slowly I began to let go. I realized I could not do it on my own. And when I met Debbie, everything became increasingly clear. I was 28 years old when we met. We should have met earlier when we were both supposed to be in the same wedding party; however, she had just given birth to Eric, so her plans to participate in the wedding had changed dramatically. Sometime later, a friend and I were having a gigantic Halloween party, and Debbie came by with some friends. She was the devil in a blue dress and I was a gorilla, with a gorilla head and gorilla chest with a yellow clown-colored jacket with prints all over it. We got introduced and spent the rest of the night talking. We began dating and I met her son, Eric, soon after. We married two years after we met. From that point on, I had not just myself to take care of, but also Eric and Debbie. I grew up a little bit. Around three years later, our son JoJo was born.

I wanted to support my family. I wanted to be there for my sons. So I created an environment where balance is not only possible, it is the rule. I could have opened my first restaurant sooner, made it a smaller place and invested less money. But I wanted to set it up right. I wanted Seastar to be a place where I could invest in the right people — people I had personally mentored at other restaurants. And I wanted to bring them to a place where we could all have a *life* as opposed to a *restaurant life*. I grew up in kitchens, often working seven days a week, 16 hours a day. I know this can be the norm. But not in my kitchens. When I opened my first restaurant, I gave my managers and chefs ownership positions in the business so they were vested. And to this day, most of my original team is still working with me.

Balance is a huge part of it. I work with each manager or chef and their individual needs. We make it possible for some people to come in early so they can leave in the afternoon to pick up their kids from school. Not only do I have a life, but the people who work with me have lives, too. When I look back over the years, it's incredible to see that we have added over 20 kids and several grandkids to our family, our restaurant family. I have watched them grow up. Many of my crew have started families, become homeowners, and I'm grateful to have been a part of these accomplishments in their lives. They know I am going to support them when it comes to family versus a business issue. Today I can spend time with my older son, Eric, and play with my first grandson, Zac. And I make it to the majority of my son JoJo's baseball games. I've even had time to coach. And watching my son on the field is, for me, a dream come true.

JoJo was recently interviewed in the local paper. He is an excellent ballplayer and has overcome a lot. In this particular news article, the reporter wrote about JoJo and his teammates and all they have endured to get to the state playoffs. In addition to working through his muscular dystrophy, JoJo had elbow surgery that would have slowed many players down. Speaking of my son and some of his teammates, the coach said, "It shows the character they have to persevere. When they want something bad enough, they just keep working." But I think my son said it best. When asked about the challenges he faced, he told the reporter, "All of us have battled through stuff before, so it's not like a shock to us. It's not like a foreign language. We knew what we had to do."

I love that I can learn from my own sons. And I am happy that I can still teach them a thing or two. Earlier this year I had the privilege of being asked to represent the state of Washington at the Democratic Governors Association's "Taste of America Gala" in Washington, D.C. The dinner was presented in conjunction with the national nonprofit hunger charity Share Our Strength, and a number of top U.S. chefs were invited to cook. I took JoJo along so he could learn about our government, as well as the issue of childhood hunger. Share Our Strength is sponsoring the "No Kid Hungry" campaign, trying to end childhood hunger in this country. As a chef, I have always been drawn to the issue of hunger. As a father and grandfather, I find the topic of childhood hunger especially potent. I have never been in a position where food was unavailable.

I've seen what hunger looks like. Every year we shut down Seastar so we can serve Thanksgiving dinner to low-income families in our community. It's probably my favorite day of the year. To see these people file into the restaurant and see the smiles spread across their faces before the food is even served — this is a gift. My staff, friends and family donate their time. We serve hundreds of people a Thanksgiving dinner. It has been our tradition for the past eight years. Every year before service starts, we all gather in the dining room and join hands, thank God and remember why we are here. To serve others. For me, it's just the right thing to do.

GRATITUDE

I HAVE A SPECIAL RELATIONSHIP with all of my restaurant partners, but I want to offer a note of gratitude to one in particular. Erik Liedholm has been more than a partner; he is a close friend and confidant whose opinions and ideas are paramount in my decision-making process.

It's funny how our relationship began. I wanted Seastar to have the best wine program in the Northwest, and I thought I had the right guy to do it. Problem was, that guy liked living in San Francisco and had no intention of returning to the Seattle area.

So I was on the hunt. And everyone I asked, the same name came up — Erik Liedholm, you have to get Erik Liedholm. So I made contact with Erik and after agreeing to his funny little list of demands (his words, not mine), and it really wasn't that little, we became partners.

After 10 years I still look at our partnership as one of the best moves I made. Erik's philosophy was that people should drink the wine they love with the food they love. That they should not feel intimidated by wine or sommeliers, that they should be comfortable with wine. I loved the idea, and Erik brought it to life. And our wine program flourished, receiving immediate accolades that included "Best New Wine List in America" from *Food & Wine* magazine.

He makes wine approachable and comfortable, not stuffy or snobby. His recommendations are so user friendly, from specific wines to varietal options, that readers will enjoy his insights.

Erik brings life to our restaurants, from his amazing sense of humor — he can do impressions of anyone (still can't get him to do me in front of me) — to his incredibly funny poems, skits and quips that he shares at every crew meeting or special occasion. Erik, from your eye for detail, to your passion for food, wine and the education of our crew, to the foreword in this very book, I can't thank you enough. I'm happy that you are my business partner and friend. Here's to the last 10 years — and many, many more.

Thank you!

FOOD AND WINE: THIS SOMMELIER'S PERSPECTIVE

Enjoying a beautifully prepared meal and a great bottle of wine with good friends is civilization at its best. Indeed, it's the epitome of La Dolce Vita. It evokes a sense of well-being around the table, and no, not always because of the alcohol in the wine. It's the sort of unexplainable, euphoric pleasure that could transform a table of scornful, dour puritans into warmhearted conversationalists at *Babette's Feast*.

There are many wine professionals who can analytically explain why certain chemical reactions occur in the mouth or hypothesize as to why a combination of food and wine did or did not work. So rather than a periodic table of chemicals, flow charts and a long list of rules, I will give you a couple of guidelines that will hopefully encourage you to create your own "euphoric" food and wine experience.

The most important "rule" that I will give to you is "Drink the wine you love with the food you love." The rest will take care of itself. Think of this whole food-and-wine synergy thing as a balancing act. Body balancing! It's matching the size and weight of the wine with the richness and intensity of the food. For example, with a hearty beef stew most of us instinctively pass up a delicate white for a flavorful red. Why? We're trying to balance the body and intensity of the wine with the same elements in the food.

To that end, consider these six attributes in wine that affect the way it tastes with food.

1) Tannin: The natural astringency in red wine that is a result of the skins, stems and seeds is neutralized by fats and oils. No wonder a big porterhouse tastes so good with a big cab.

2) Acid: Not in the '60s and '70s psychedelic sense. Look for foods with complementary acids. Seek out delicate foods and make sure the wine has as much acidity as or more than the accompanying dish.

3) Alcohol: Avoid salty foods. Salt will make wines that have a high percentage of alcohol taste bitter.

4) Sweetness: Think of wines with a bit of residual sugar as a little fire extinguisher for fiery, aggressive foods.

5) Temperature: An often overlooked attribute. When white wine is served too cold, the flavor is muted, and when red wine is served too cold, the tannin is accentuated.

6) Aim carefully: Make sure you are targeting the most prominent flavor and texture on the plate to match the wine with. Most often it's not the main ingredient.

Alas, even with this minor bit of rule making, I see an inherent danger in taking it too seriously. One could get the impression that good food and wine matches are impossible without this fussing around. Nothing could be further from the truth. Just follow my only rule — "Drink the wine you love with the food you love" — and you are well on your way to euphoria!

ERIK LIEDHOLM
PARTNER
COMPANY WINE DIRECTOR - ADVANCED SOMMELIER
JOHN HOWIE RESTAURANT GROUP

Notes about the Recipes, Process and Ingredients

Before you start a recipe, it is helpful to read through it. If the recipe asks for a preheated oven, make sure the oven is preheated at the specific temperature before starting.

You will find that the recipes have exact measurements. This is done to ensure that the flavor profiles desired for the recipe are correct. You will also find that some ingredients are specified to very exact cuts. This is also done to ensure that the flavor profiles are correct. It may at times seem a little over the top, but that's what I intended.

Some people prefer to have their recipes state: "Dice 1 Roma tomato." I prefer to list the exact amount by cups or tablespoons because not all Roma tomatoes or other produce items are the same size, and size variance will change the flavor profile of the recipe. This means that you may have to estimate how much you'll need to produce the listed ingredient amount.

Many of my recipes are very explicit as to the cut size of the ingredient. There is a big difference between the flavor profile of an onion that is diced ½ inch and one that is diced ¼ inch or one that is minced, and it affects the flavor of the finished dish. So that is why all the chefs in my restaurants carry a ruler and frequently check their cutting specifications. It helps make what we do consistent.

If you don't like something, don't add it. I have always said that people should eat what they like or what they enjoy. It is not blasphemy to change a recipe, to delete something you don't like or add something you do. What is most important is that you like what you have created — so have fun with it!

Caramelization – This is a term used to describe the level that foods have been cooked to, referring to the golden caramel color.

Deglaze – Deglaze is the term used for adding a liquid to a hot pan after food has been sautéed, then stirring that liquid to remove any caramelization that has formed on the bottom of the pan, releasing those flavors into the dish.

How to Cook Pasta – Dry pasta should be cooked in boiling water, with no salt and no oil. When it is removed from the water, never rinse the pasta. This washes away some of the natural starch, which will help thicken the sauce. Rinsing also causes the pasta to absorb water and lose its texture.

If the pasta is going to be used immediately, it should be cooked al dente, with a texture that is slightly firm but not crisp. If it is going to be cooked again later, it should be cooked only until it is very firm, with a slightly crisp bite.

If the pasta is to be used immediately, the sauce will keep it from clumping. If you are not using the pasta immediately, drizzle it with a little olive oil and toss to coat. Then spread it on a sheet tray to cool at room temperature, never layered more than ½ inch thick.

Mangoes – There is a very large fibrous seed in the center of a mango; it runs from top to bottom in the same oval shape as the mango. To get the meat out of a mango, cut a quarter-sized slice off the stem end, look to see the seed's position, and stand the mango up on the cut end. Using a very sharp knife, cut as close to the seed as possible, slicing off the fat sides of the mango. Then cut off the remaining slices as close to the seed as possible. Next slice the inside of the mango in a crisscross pattern, then fold the skin inside out and the mango chunks will be accessible.

To peel a mango, use the same technique, but instead of cutting off the sides, just shave off the skin and then remove chunks from the fat sides of the mango.

A ripe mango should have a sweet smell and have a slightly tender spot when touched at the stem, but still be firm. Mangoes can be ripened in a day or two when placed by a window with good sunlight.

MUSSELS – Mussels must be cleaned and debearded before they are cooked. The beard is actually the fibrous strands that keep the mussels attached to the ropes where they are grown. Grab the beard with your thumb and forefinger, pull it toward the pointed end of the mussel, and tear it off. You may have to jerk it fairly hard. Once the beard is removed, mussels will soon die, so they should be cooked within 24 hours.

ROASTED GARLIC CLOVES – Several of the recipes require a roasted garlic clove as opposed to just roasted garlic. These can be made from fresh peeled whole cloves, tossed in olive oil and placed on a cookie sheet or roasting pan in a 350°F oven for 8 to 12 minutes, until golden brown.

To peel the cloves, crush with a knife and remove the skin. Or wear rubber gloves and roll the cloves between your hands; the skin will come off, leaving the cloves whole — a method I prefer.

ROASTED PEPPERS – When a recipe calls for roasted peppers, they will always have to be peeled and seeded. Peppers can be roasted several ways: in an oven at 450°F or higher, on a gas or charcoal outdoor grill, or on a gas stovetop directly over the flame. In all cases you want to cook the pepper until it has softened and much of the exterior skin is charred. When using the flame method, you must turn the pepper every 1 to 2 minutes. Remove the peppers from the heat source and let cool slightly. While they are still warm, place in a plastic bag and seal. When they are cool, remove the skin. It should come off easily in large strips.

STEAK GRILLING – When grilling steaks, I like to leave them out at room temperature to temper. This allows for much more even cooking, as the center of the steak is not cold. For large groups, at times I will presear the steaks in pans to seal in the juices and then let them sit out at room temperature before finishing them in the oven. The searing process helps warm the interior of the steak and melt the fats, which makes the steak juicier.

STOCK – When making stock, it is always going to be easier to produce more than you'll need for an individual recipe. Leftover stock can be portioned into ice-cube trays or plastic containers and frozen, and can be held for several months.

ZEST – When a recipe calls for zest, it is referring to the outer layer of a citrus fruit — a lemon, lime, orange or any other citrus. The key to good flavorful zest is to use only the outer layer of the skin and none of the white fleshy part. The colorful outer layer is where the aromatic citrus oils reside. The white part just beneath it is bitter. As taste comes from your sense of smell as well as your taste buds, the oils from the zest enhance the flavor of citrus in my recipes. Zest can be minced very fine, or shaved with a Microplane, or used in fine strips.

NOTES ON INGREDIENTS

ANCHOVIES – While I prefer to use whole anchovies in the recipes, I understand that you may not be able to use the leftover anchovies. Anchovy paste can be substituted.

BLACK TRUFFLES – Black truffles are expensive and hard to find. Restaurants here are lucky to have an opportunity to purchase fresh local black truffles from November through April. When they are not available, we will choose to use frozen truffles first, then jarred or canned. If black truffles are unavailable, you can increase the amount of truffle-infused olive oil to help boost the truffle flavor in the recipes.

CLARIFIED BUTTER – Many of the recipes call for clarified butter because I enjoy the rich flavor as opposed to that of many oils. You can also use a product called ghee, which is a form of clarified butter.

EGGS – At all of my restaurants, we use cage-free eggs — not only for the humane treatment of the birds, but also for the quality and flavor of the egg. Wherever eggs are called for in the recipes, they should be cage-free organic.

FISH FILLETS – The blood line of the fish fillet is on the skin side of the fish and usually runs down the middle. It is dark red or brown and has a much stronger, not completely pleasant flavor, which is why we remove it from our fish portions. Block cut refers to a fillet of fish that has been cut to the shape of a square or a rectangle, with an even thickness throughout. This allows the fish to cook evenly. Usually it is 3 to 4 inches long, 2 to 3 inches wide, and 1 to 2 inches thick.

FISH SELECTION AND STORAGE – Fish selection is an important part of creating great fish dishes. Whenever possible, purchase your fish from a market where you can smell the fish before you buy it. Fish should always smell like a fresh salty sea breeze. It should never have a strong fishy odor. The flesh should be bright and shiny; dull fish with mealy-looking flesh is old. When buying whole fish, look at the eyes — they should still be clear and bright, not cloudy. When holding fish for more than eight hours before use, keep it very cold, as close to 32°F as possible. Place the fish in a perforated pan, with a drip pan beneath it. Cover the fish with plastic wrap and then cover the plastic wrap with ice. If the fish is skinless, don't let the ice directly touch it, as it will damage the flesh.

Fish, scallops, shrimp, crab and other shellfish will deteriorate more quickly than other proteins when not properly cooled. This affects the quality and the safety of the seafood.

FRESH HERBS – Many of my recipes call for fresh herbs. If you're buying them, there will usually be more than you need. This is a good thing. Fresh herbs can be used in many different ways. You can make your own infused oils or vinegars by immersing them in oil or vinegar and letting their flavor seep in. You can also hang them and turn them into dried herbs. When you purchase fresh herbs, cut off the bottoms of the stems and place the herbs in a glass of cold water in the refrigerator. They will hold like this for at least four to five days. Then repeat the process and they will hold for another three to four days. Many people now are growing herbs in pots to use in their kitchens. They are beautiful and hardy plants that need little care.

GRANULATED GARLIC AND ONION – The recipes often call for dry granulated garlic or onion. This is not the same as powdered. Garlic or onion powder is extremely fine, while granulated has some coarse texture, although at times I have found granulated garlic or onion sold as powdered. What I consider powdered would be similar in consistency to powdered sugar.

LEEKS – Leeks are very large, mild onions. Most of the flavor comes from the lighter green or white parts. But the green tops can be used in making stocks. To clean a leek, pull the layers apart, rinse thoroughly, dry, and chop.

PEAR TOMATOES IN JUICE – The best canned pear tomatoes in juice are San Marzanos. I recommend using these whenever possible, but most pear or plum tomatoes in juice will suffice.

POTATO GNOCCHI – There is a recipe included, but to make it easy, there are also many high-quality fresh potato gnocchi products available in grocery stores.

PRESERVED LEMONS – These can be used to season many different dishes, from relishes and dressings to seafood and poultry. They add a very bright and salty lemon flavor.

RICOTTA SALATA – This is best used in salads, but can also be used in a baked pasta dish. It is a firm, dry cheese with a mild flavor and grainy texture.

SALTS – Sea salts are the best salt to use on finished dishes, as they have a nice crisp texture and mild flavor. My favorite is Australian Pink Sea Salt from Murray River, but a close second, especially for steaks, is the Black Lava Sea Salt from Hawaii, then either French or Portuguese fleur de sel. I find that when using salts for seasoning larger-batch recipes, kosher salt works very well and is much more cost efficient. There are several different brands of kosher salt, with varying degrees of density, which changes the salt content dramatically. I recommend using only Diamond kosher salt, as it is soft, flaky and light-flavored. All of my recipes have been designed to use this product. If you use Morton's, use half as much. Other kosher salts may be too heavy and will change the flavor of the dish. If you can't get Diamond brand, use a flaky sea salt, or make sure to add a little at a time and taste often.

SWEET ONIONS – Many of the recipes call for Walla Walla sweets or Maui sweet onions. Any white or yellow sweet onion can be substituted.

TOMATOES – Tomatoes are best stored and served at room temperature, especially for salads. The flavor of the tomato is much less prominent when it is chilled.

WHITE GULF SHRIMP – Most of my recipes specify using white Gulf shrimp. I think they have the best flavor. Black tiger prawns are a good substitute.

KITCHEN TOOLS

CEDAR BAKING PLANKS – Alder and Cedar Baking Planks and Cedar Barbecue Grilling Planks, as well as Chef Howie's 3 Chefs in a Tub Spice Rubs and Seasoning Blends, are available at www.plankcooking.com or Seastar Restaurant and Raw Bar.

Our cedar planks are a great tool for making healthy, low-fat, high-flavor foods. The cooking is simple, as you will see in the recipe provided. Cedar planks help to maintain the moisture of the foods that are cooked on them; a subtle wood flavor is imparted into the foods so they don't need a lot of seasonings or butter. The foods take a little longer to cook, but that also means there is more room for error — if the foods cook on the plank a little too long, they are still moist and tender. They maintain moisture even in hard-to-cook foods like boneless, skinless chicken breast or lean fish like halibut.

The Cedar Baking Planks can be used over and over again for years, while the Cedar BBQ Planks are for one-time use. The baking planks are always used in an indoor conventional oven. They don't have to be soaked in water, as they are never exposed to live flame. The BBQ planks are always soaked in water for a minimum of one to two hours, as they are exposed to live flames on the grill and are encouraged to catch fire, providing a rich smoky flavor to the foods that are cooked on them.

CONVECTION OVEN – Today many people have a convection oven option on their ovens. The convection oven cooks more evenly, as it moves the warm air around the food being baked or roasted, browning the items better. If you want to use a convection oven with the recipes here, reduce the temperature by 25°F. This should even out the cooking temperature, so the timing will remain the same.

JAPANESE MANDOLINE – The Japanese mandoline is an inexpensive option (plastic with metal blades) used to make fine julienne and thinly shaved vegetables. It's a great time-saving tool. They can be found at most Asian markets.

SILPAT – This is a reusable nonstick baking sheet that you use instead of parchment paper or greasing a pan. It is great for baking cookies or other sticky baked goods.

SMALL FOOD PROCESSOR – A two-cup Cuisinart food processor is a must for any kitchen. They are efficient, easy to clean, and perfect for making small batches. They can usually be found at kitchen stores or Costco.

SPICE GRINDER – Grinding your own spices or dried herbs can add a lot of flavor to your foods. I use a small portable coffee grinder for my herbs and spices; it works well and is an inexpensive tool. Any department store should have one.

SQUEEZE BOTTLE – Many recipes call for a squeeze bottle. These are used to decorate plates with sauces. The squeeze bottle is basically a clear "ketchup bottle," so you can see which sauce it contains. They can also be used as storage containers. They are usually around $1 at kitchen stores.

THERMOMETER – The best way to measure internal temperature is with a 0-220°F cooking thermometer.

Specialty Ingredients

ALAEA SEA SALT – A Hawaiian sea salt with a red-orange clay tint. It can be found at specialty food stores or kitchen stores.

BLACK TRUFFLES – A very pungent fungus that looks like a black rock. Imported black truffles are very expensive ($500-$800 per pound); local truffles are still expensive but more reasonable ($120-$150 per pound). Canned or jarred truffles are not nearly as flavorful. The best places to find them are specialty food stores or farmers' markets, from local foragers.

KAFFIR LIME LEAF – The very fragrant and flavorful leaf of the kaffir lime tree. Used primarily in Thai cooking, it is best if fresh or flash frozen; do not use dried. It can be found online through Thai specialty food providers, or even at Amazon.com.

LEMONGRASS – A long stem consisting of many layers, with the flavor of lemon oil. Remove the exterior layers, which are very fibrous and tasteless. Use only the lighter interior layers, which are tender and flavorful. Leftover lemongrass can be chopped and dried or powdered to add flavor to mainly Thai dishes.

OGO – Fresh Hawaiian seaweed with the flavor of fresh seawater. It is used in making poke. It is available at Asian markets. Frozen can also be used.

OPAL BASIL – A purple/burgundy-colored basil with ruffled leaves. Thai basil can be substituted, as they are similar in flavor. Thai basil has a purple stem with a green leaf similar to sweet basil, except the leaves are heartier.

PICKAPEPPA SAUCE – A spicy Jamaican sauce made from mango, onion, raisins, spices, tamarind and cane vinegar.

QUAIL EGGS – Small eggs that can be used in tartare preparations, as well as salads. They can be found in specialty food stores, at a reasonable price. Extras can be boiled and pickled.

SAMBAL OELEK – A very spicy red chili paste. It can be found at Asian markets.

THAI CURRY PASTE (OR MALAYSIAN) – A very spicy curry flavoring, with additional seasonings, used in Thai cooking. It can be found at Asian markets.

THAI FISH SAUCE – A very strong fish flavoring used in Thai cooking. This inexpensive ingredient can be found at Asian markets.

TOGARASHI SEASONING – A Japanese chili seasoning blend. It can be found at Asian markets.

TRUFFLE OIL – An easy and less expensive way to add truffle flavor to your dishes. I like white-truffle-infused olive oils, as they are usually more fragrant. They are not cheap, but relatively inexpensive in comparison to truffles.

WET JERK – A Jamaican marinade. There is a recipe for it in the book, and it will keep for several months. But it can sometimes be purchased. The best I have found was Busha Browne's.

WHEAT BERRIES – The entire wheat kernels except the husk. When cooked, they hold their shape and have a firm yet tender texture with a full wheat flavor.

APPETIZERS

STEAMED CLAMS WITH PESTO
SERVES 4

2 tablespoons olive oil
1½ teaspoons minced fresh garlic
½ teaspoon crushed red pepper flakes
¼ cup dry white wine
2 pounds clams in the shell, scrubbed – small Manila or butter clams
½ cup Basil Pesto
2 tablespoons pine nuts, toasted (page 73)
8 shavings Parmigiano-Reggiano cheese

Heat the olive oil in a large sauté pan over medium heat. Add the garlic and red pepper, and sauté for 1 to 2 minutes, or until the garlic begins to turn golden.

Add the wine and stir to deglaze the pan. When the liquid begins to boil, add the clams. Reduce the heat to low and cover. Cook for 2 to 3 minutes, or until the clams just begin to open.

Add the pesto and cook briefly, until the sauce just begins to thicken. Transfer to a heated bowl. Garnish with the pine nuts and shaved Parmigiano.

BASIL PESTO
MAKES 1 CUP

½ cup packed coarsely chopped fresh basil
¼ cup coarsely chopped fresh Italian parsley
1 tablespoon minced fresh garlic
¼ cup pine nuts, toasted (page 73)
½ teaspoon kosher salt
3 tablespoons grated Parmigiano-Reggiano cheese
2 tablespoons salted butter
⅓ cup olive oil

After you have made fresh pesto, it immediately starts to oxidize and turn a darker color. To ensure freshness, place the pesto in a container, press it down, top it with a layer of olive oil, and seal the container. It will keep in the refrigerator for two to three days.

In a food processor, combine the basil, parsley, garlic, pine nuts, salt and grated cheese. Pulse until the ingredients are finely chopped but not pureed to mush. Then add the butter and oil, and process until a thick paste forms.

WINE:
The "life is too short" pick:
La Spinetta, Vermentino, Tuscany, Italy 2009
The "just because it's inexpensive doesn't mean you're cheap" pick:
Corte Giara, Pinot Grigio, Veneto, Italy 2009
Alternatives: *Crisp white wine with a ripe fruit edge. Albariño from Spain or dry Pinot Gris from Oregon.*

Thai Coconut Curry Mussels

Yield: 4 appetizer servings
½ cup Thai Broth
1½ pounds fresh mussels, debearded (page 23)
2 tablespoons julienne-sliced red bell peppers
      (1-by-¼-by-¼-inch slices)
1 tablespoon diagonally sliced green onion
      (⅛-inch pieces)
½ cup Coconut-Curry Slurry
½ lime, cut into 4 wedges
1 tablespoon thinly sliced opal or Thai dark
      purple basil
4 large fresh cilantro sprigs

Yield: 4 entrée servings
1 cup Thai Broth
3 pounds fresh mussels, debearded (page 23)
¼ cup julienne-sliced red bell peppers
      (1-by-¼-by-¼-inch slices)
2 tablespoons diagonally sliced green onion
      (⅛-inch pieces)
1 cup Coconut-Curry Slurry
½ lime, cut into 4 wedges
2 tablespoons thinly sliced opal or Thai dark
      purple basil
4 large fresh cilantro sprigs

Thai Broth
Makes 2 cups
2 cups Vegetable Stock (page 118)
2 kaffir lime leaves
2 tablespoons sliced lemongrass – interior
      white part only, cut in half lengthwise
      and sliced into ⅛-inch pieces
2 teaspoons Mae Ploy Thai chili paste in oil
1 teaspoon red curry paste
1 teaspoon sambal oelek (chili paste)
1 fresh Thai chile, cut in half lengthwise

Coconut-Curry Slurry
Makes 1 cup
1 cup coconut milk
1 teaspoon Thai or Malaysian curry powder
      (Indian can be substituted)
1½ teaspoons arrowroot (or cornstarch)

Prepare the Thai Broth: Place all the ingredients in a stockpot and heat until boiling, then reduce the heat to very low and simmer for 45 minutes. Remove the Thai chile. Let cool, then refrigerate until needed.

Prepare the Coconut-Curry Slurry: Combine all the ingredients and mix until well blended. Refrigerate until needed.

To prepare the mussels, stir the broth well and place in a sauté pan. Warm over medium heat, then add the mussels, cover, and cook until the mussels have opened, about 1½ to 3 minutes, depending on the variety of mussel. Add the bell peppers and green onions.

Stir the slurry vigorously to incorporate the arrowroot, then add it to the broth. Let simmer for 30 seconds, until it thickens slightly. It should be the consistency of whipping cream.

Place the mussels and liquid in a bowl, standing up some of the mussels. Squeeze the lime over the mussels. Garnish with the basil and cilantro sprigs.

Wine:
The "life is too short" pick:
Poet's Leap, Riesling, Columbia Valley, Washington 2009
The "just because it's inexpensive doesn't mean you're cheap" pick:
Covey Run, Riesling, Columbia Valley, Washington 2009
Alternatives: *A white wine that has a bit of residual sugar to balance the heat of the dish. German "QbA"*
      or Spätlese Riesling or Chenin Blanc (Vouvray) from France.

MUSSELS PROVENÇAL
SERVES 2

2 tablespoons olive oil

1 tablespoon shaved whole garlic cloves

2 tablespoons finely minced white onion

1½ pounds mussels in the shell (preferably large Penn Cove mussels), scrubbed
 and debearded (page 23)

1 cup diced heirloom tomato (½-inch pieces)

¾ teaspoon sea salt

½ teaspoon freshly ground pepper

1 tablespoon clam juice blended with 1 tablespoon dry white wine

1 tablespoon plus 1 teaspoon coarsely chopped fresh Italian parsley

SERVES 4

4 tablespoons olive oil

2 tablespoons shaved whole garlic cloves

¼ cup finely minced white onion

3 pounds mussels in the shell (preferably large Penn Cove mussels), scrubbed
 and debearded (page 23)

2 cups diced heirloom tomato (½-inch pieces)

1½ teaspoons sea salt

1 teaspoon freshly ground pepper

2 tablespoons clam juice blended with 2 tablespoons dry white wine

2 tablespoons plus 2 teaspoons coarsely chopped fresh Italian parsley

Heat the olive oil in a 12-inch sauté pan over medium-high heat.
If you are making 4 servings, it is better to use 2 sauté pans.
When the oil is beginning to heat but not smoke, add the garlic
and onion. Sauté until the garlic is turning golden.

Add the mussels to the pan and toss lightly. Add the tomatoes,
salt and pepper. Cook and toss for 1 minute, then add the clam
juice/wine blend. Lower the heat to medium, cover, and steam
for 2 to 3 minutes, or until the mussels have opened.

Add the parsley and toss lightly. Place in individual bowls or
a serving bowl, with some of the garlic, onion and tomatoes on
top. Serve with baguette toasts.

> **WINE:**
> The "life is too short" pick:
> ***Domaine Tempier, Rosé, Bandol, France 2010***
> The "just because it's inexpensive doesn't mean you're cheap" pick:
> ***Château d'Esclans, Rosé, "Whispering Angel," Provence, France 2010***
> Alternatives: *Virtually any Rosé (not white Zinfandel, unless you love it) that has been
> produced within one vintage of the current year.*

OYSTERS WITH MELON RELISH
SERVES 4

1½ cups crushed ice or rock salt, slightly moistened, chilled to 32°F (see note)
12 fresh oysters in the shell, scrubbed, shucked and detached
1 large fresh Italian parsley sprig

MELON RELISH
¼ cup diced ripe seedless watermelon (¼-inch pieces)
¼ cup diced ripe honeydew melon (¼-inch pieces)
¼ cup diced ripe cantaloupe (¼-inch pieces)
1½ teaspoons diced lemon – skin and membrane removed, no seeds, ¼-inch pieces
1½ teaspoons shallots sliced paper-thin
½ teaspoon champagne vinegar

Prepare the Melon Relish: Combine all the ingredients and mix until blended.
Chill for at least 2 hours before using.

To serve, place the crushed ice or chilled rock salt on a platter. Make 12
indentations in the ice. Place 1 tablespoon of the relish on top of each oyster in
the shell (for smaller oysters, reduce the relish amount to 2 teaspoons per oyster),
and place each oyster on the ice. Garnish with the parsley sprig.

Note: To chill rock salt, place in the freezer for 45 to 60 minutes.

Note: Different kinds of melon can be substituted, especially in the late summer when local
heirloom varieties are available. The key is to make sure that your melons are ripe and sweet, no
matter which ones you use.

Cleaning oysters: Whether you pick them off the beach yourself or buy them at Pike Place Market,
oysters should be cleaned. Simply run cold water over the shells and rub with your hands to remove
any sand or mud; if you have sensitive hands, wear dishwashing gloves. Then refrigerate, cup shell
side down, until needed. To shuck an oyster, use an oyster knife that feels good in your hand;
I like to use a short thick-bladed oyster knife. Place the tip of the knife in the small slot between the
top and bottom shell at the hinge of the oyster and work the tip into the slot. Once the tip is firmly
implanted in the slot, twist the knife slowly. You should hear a slight pop when the oyster's muscle
seal is broken. Run the knife along the outside edge of the shell to completely dislodge the top
shell. Next, carefully run the knife beneath the oyster to cut the bottom muscle seal, being sure not
to puncture the stomach. Remove any small shell chips. Refrigerate, covered, until needed, or serve
immediately.

WINE:
The "life is too short" pick:
Domaine de la Grange, "Clos des Allées," Muscadet, Loire, France 2009
The "just because it's inexpensive doesn't mean you're cheap" pick:
Laurent Bossis, Muscadet, Loire, France 2010
Alternatives: *A super-crisp and high-acid white wine with minerality. Delicacy and freshness of the
oyster balanced by the delicacy and freshness of the wine. Vinho Verde from Portugal
or New Zealand Sauvignon Blanc.*

FRESH SHUCKED OYSTERS WITH POMEGRANATE-CITRUS RELISH
SERVES 4

1½ cups rock salt, slightly moistened, chilled to 32°F (see note)
12 fresh oysters in the shell, scrubbed and shucked (page 33)
1 fresh Italian parsley sprig

POMEGRANATE-CITRUS RELISH
2 tablespoons fresh pink or red grapefruit cut into ½-inch pieces
3 tablespoons fresh mandarin orange cut into ½-inch pieces
1 tablespoon Meyer lemon cut into ½-inch pieces
2 tablespoons pomegranate seeds
1½ teaspoons very, very thinly sliced shallot (paper thin)
¼ teaspoon champagne vinegar

Prepare the Pomegranate-Citrus Relish: Combine all the ingredients and mix until well blended.
Refrigerate for at least 2 hours before using, and up to 36 hours.

To serve, place the chilled rock salt on a platter. Make 12 indentations in the rock salt. Place
2 teaspoons of the relish on top of each oyster in the shell. Place the oysters on the rock salt
and garnish with the parsley sprig.

Note: To chill rock salt, place in the freezer for 45 to 60 minutes.

Oysters come in many different sizes for many different uses — small, medium, large, yearling. For raw consumption
I prefer a smaller oyster, a Kumamoto, a Kusshi or even the smallest oyster, the Olympia, which is bred and harvested
at a very petite size. For raw consumption, most people prefer what is referred to as a yearling oyster, which is actually
slightly smaller than a small oyster. Small, medium and large oysters are usually used for cooking. I still prefer to use the
small for fried oysters, as the medium and especially the large oysters can get to sizes over 6 inches long.

They say that oysters are best in the months that end in "er," but that's not completely true. Why stay away? Well, there
are actually two good reasons. When the water warms up, the oysters enter their reproduction stage, which makes them
soft and milky, and they just don't taste that great. The preferred texture is firm and briny. The other reason is red tide,
a summer-blooming phytoplankton algae that can make you ill if ingested. So it is best to enjoy our local oysters from
September through April or even May if the waters stay cool.

That doesn't mean you can't eat oysters during the summer months; they just have to come from colder waters. Prince
Edward Island has a variety called the Malpeque that is usually very good in the summer, and Chilean oysters are also
good during the summer months. Locally, they are growing some oysters in deep colder waters, and the triploid oyster
stays firm and briny through the summer season.

WINE:
The "life is too short" pick:
Duval-Leroy, Rosé, Vertus, France
The "just because it's inexpensive doesn't mean you're cheap" pick:
Louis Bouillot, Crémant de Bourgogne, Rosé, France
Alternatives: *A crisp sparkling wine with a rich fruit core. Champagne Rosé or a California sparkling wine.*

OYSTERS WITH CREAMED LEEKS AND ASIAGO
SERVES 4

12 extra-small Pacific oysters
1 teaspoon sea or kosher salt
1 teaspoon freshly ground black pepper
¼ cup freshly grated Asiago cheese
Rock salt, for serving (see note)
1 fresh thyme sprig

CREAMED LEEKS

1 tablespoon plus 1½ teaspoons canola or olive oil
¼ teaspoon minced fresh garlic
½ cup sliced leeks, white and light green parts only, sliced in half and then in ¼-inch pieces
    (see note)
1½ teaspoons flour
¼ cup Chicken Stock (page 120)
½ teaspoon minced fresh thyme
6 tablespoons whipping cream

Prepare the Creamed Leeks: Heat the oil in a sauté pan over medium heat. Add the garlic and sauté lightly until translucent.

Add the leeks and sauté until tender. Add the flour and cook, stirring, for 30 to 45 seconds to create a roux. Then add the chicken broth, stirring to deglaze the pan. Add the thyme. Let simmer and reduce slightly.

Add the cream and cook until slightly reduced. Let cool, then refrigerate until needed.

Shuck the oysters and clean the shells. In the cup side of each shell, place 1 tablespoon of creamed leeks.

Then place the oyster on the creamed leeks, and season with the salt and pepper. Top each oyster with 1 teaspoon of grated Asiago. Refrigerate until needed.

To serve: Preheat the oven to 475°F.

Place the oysters on a baking tray and set in the oven. Bake until the cheese has browned and the sauce is bubbling, approximately 6 to 7 minutes. Place on a bed of oven-warmed rock salt. Garnish with the thyme sprig.

Note: To warm the rock salt, place in a 325°F oven for 15 to 20 minutes.

Note: Leeks are often very dirty, so be sure to wash them thoroughly.

WINE:
    The "life is too short" pick:
    Krug, Grand Cuvée, Reims, France
    The "just because it's inexpensive doesn't mean you're cheap" pick:
    Lucien Albrecht, Crément d'Alsace, France
    Alternatives: *A crisp and elegant sparkling wine to balance the richness of the dish and lift the delicate*
    flavors of the oysters. Cava from Spain or sparkling wine from California.

HAWAIIAN AHI POKE
SERVES 4

8 ounces fresh sashimi-grade ahi tuna, cut into ½-inch chunks, well chilled
¾ teaspoon finely minced fresh garlic
4½ teaspoons cleaned ogo (fresh seaweed) cut into ¼-inch pieces
⅓ cup quartered and sliced Maui sweet onion (⅛-inch slices)
¾ teaspoon sesame seeds, toasted
2 tablespoons light soy sauce
1½ teaspoons toasted sesame oil
¼ teaspoon crushed red pepper flakes
½ ounce daikon sprouts
½ cup finely shredded fresh daikon
⅛ teaspoon togarashi (a spicy Japanese seasoning blend)
12 to 16 crispy taro chips or black pepper crackers

Mix together the tuna, garlic, ogo, onion and sesame seeds.

In a small bowl, blend the soy sauce, sesame oil and red pepper. Toss with the ahi mixture until well coated.

Place the daikon sprouts on the back side of individual plates or a serving dish, and top with a mound of shredded daikon. Place the poke on the front side of the shredded daikon, slightly overlapping it. Garnish the top of the poke with togarashi seasoning.

Serve the chips or crackers on the side.

WINE:
The "life is too short" pick:
Cloudy Bay, Sauvignon Blanc, Marlborough, New Zealand 2010
The "just because it's inexpensive doesn't mean you're cheap" pick:
Dashwood, Sauvignon Blanc, Marlborough, New Zealand 2010
Alternatives: *Dry white wine with citrus and herbal notes. Albariño from Spain or California Sauvignon Blanc.*

SEARED AHI WITH NEW POTATO CHIPS

SERVES 4

4 pieces block-cut sashimi-grade ahi tuna,
        3 ounces each
2 teaspoons olive oil
4 teaspoons Herb Crust
2 tablespoons plus 2 teaspoons Black Truffle
        Vinaigrette (page 63)

HERB CRUST

MAKES ½ CUP

2 tablespoons dried basil
2 tablespoons dried savory
1½ teaspoons dried dill
4½ teaspoons sea salt
1½ teaspoons granulated garlic
2 teaspoons granulated onion
1 teaspoon ground black pepper

NEW POTATO CHIPS

12 ounces new white potatoes, medium size
Canola oil for deep-frying
½ teaspoon sea salt
⅛ teaspoon ground black pepper

Special equipment: deep fryer

Prepare the Herb Crust: Combine all the ingredients in a spice grinder and pulse 2 to 3 times, leaving the herbs blended but still very large. Store in an airtight container at room temperature.

Prepare the New Potato Chips: Wash the potatoes, but leave the skin on. Slice very thin with a mandoline or a meat slicer, about ⅟₁₆ inch thick. Place the slices in ice-cold water and let soak for 1 hour. Remove from the water, drain, and let dry. Remove excess water with a towel. Preheat the oil in a deep fryer to 375°F.

When the oil is hot, place the potatoes in the fryer in a single layer and cook until golden brown, about 1 to 2 minutes. Remove from the fryer and place on paper towels to absorb the excess oil. Season the chips with the salt and pepper. Let cool to room temperature. Store in a sealed container at room temperature until needed.

To prepare the fish, coat each piece of ahi with ½ teaspoon olive oil. Season each piece with 1 teaspoon of the herb crust.

Heat a sauté pan over medium-high heat. Place the ahi in the pan and sear on all 4 long sides until it has a seared appearance but is still rare inside, approximately 20 to 30 seconds per side. Remove the ahi from the pan, let rest for 1 minute, and slice.

Place the ahi slices on one side of each plate and the potato chips on the other. Drizzle the vinaigrette over the ahi.

WINE:
    The "life is too short" pick:
    Nigl, Grüner Veltliner, Smaragd, Wachau, Austria 2008
    The "just because it's inexpensive doesn't mean you're cheap" pick:
    Berger, Grüner Veltliner, Kremstal, Austria 2009
    Alternatives: *A dry white wine with medium-plus acidity, minerality and ripe fruit notes to match the richness of the chips and the silkiness of the tuna. Dry Chenin Blanc from France or unoaked Sauvignon Blanc from a warm, ripe vintage.*

CLASSIC AHI TARTARE
SERVES 4

1 cup diced fresh ahi tuna (¼-inch pieces)
¼ cup minced white onion (¹⁄₁₆-inch pieces)
2 teaspoons minced capers (⅛-inch pieces)
2 teaspoons minced high-quality cured anchovy (¹⁄₁₆-inch pieces)
2 teaspoons whole-grain mustard
½ teaspoon sea salt
½ teaspoon freshly ground black pepper
2 teaspoons fresh lemon juice
1 tablespoon plus 1 teaspoon best-quality first-press extra-virgin olive oil
4 quail eggs, yolks only

Special equipment: 3-inch plastic or stainless steel ring

Combine all ingredients except the olive oil and egg yolks. Stir until well blended.

For each serving, place the plastic or stainless steel ring on a plate. Press a quarter of the tartare mix into the ring. Remove the ring, leaving a patty.

Drizzle olive oil on the plates around the patties. Top each patty with an egg yolk.

Serve with Melba toasts or toast points.

WINE:
The "life is too short" pick:
Domaine Thivin, "Brouilly," Beaujolais, France 2007
The "just because it's inexpensive doesn't mean you're cheap" pick:
Louis Jadot, Beaujolais, France 2009
Alternatives: *Fruity, low-tannin red wine with earthy notes that balances the silkiness of the dish. Dolcetto d'Alba, Italy, or a Gamay from Oregon.*

Seared Scallops with Beet Carpaccio and Black Truffle Vinaigrette
Serves 4

20 fresh sea scallops (10/20 count)
1½ teaspoons sea salt
1 teaspoon freshly ground pepper
2 tablespoons canola oil
½ pound cooked golden beets, peeled and sliced paper thin (see note)
1 cup baby arugula, stems removed
¼ cup Black Truffle Vinaigrette (page 63), divided
1½ teaspoons sliced chives (⅛-inch pieces)

Season the scallops with salt and pepper. Place the scallops on a lightly oiled seasoned flat-top grill preheated to 400-450°F, or a sauté pan over medium-high to high heat. Sear until golden brown, approximately 1 to 1½ minutes per side (see note).

Arrange the sliced beets evenly on 4 plates, slightly overlapping to cover the entire interior surface.

Toss the arugula in half of the vinaigrette. Mound the arugula in the center of each plate.

Place the scallops around the edges of each plate, sitting on top of the beets. Drizzle the remaining vinaigrette over the scallops. Top the scallops with the chives.

Note: The beets should be cooked in boiling water to an internal temperature of 140°F, then chilled, peeled, and sliced on a Japanese mandoline.

Note: The scallops should have a seared exterior but remain tender and medium-rare inside for the best flavor and texture.

WINE:
The "life is too short" pick:
Dauvissat-Camus, "La Forest," Chablis, France 2007
The "just because it's inexpensive doesn't mean you're cheap" pick:
Joseph Drouhin, Mâcon-Villages (Chardonnay), France 2009
Alternatives: *Dry, unoaked Chardonnay with medium-plus acidity and earth notes to balance the richness and earthiness of the dish.*

THAI BEEF WITH GRAPES
SERVES 4

1 cup cooked glass noodles (saifun bean
  threads) – see cooking instructions
1 pound beef tenderloin, cut into ¼-inch-thick
  by 1- to 1½-inch-wide medallions
2 tablespoons olive oil
2 tablespoons fresh lime juice
¾ cup sliced red and green grapes in equal
  amounts (⅛- to ¼-inch crosswise
  slices)
4 fresh cilantro sprigs

CORIANDER RUB
2¼ teaspoons kosher salt
1¼ teaspoons ground coriander
½ teaspoon ground black pepper

THAI NOODLE DRESSING
¾ teaspoon thinly sliced peeled fresh ginger
1½ teaspoons minced fresh garlic
1⅛ teaspoons minced lemongrass, white
  part only
⅜ teaspoon minced fresh kaffir lime leaf
1 tablespoon sugar
2¼ teaspoons Thai fish sauce
2 tablespoons plus 1½ teaspoons unseasoned
  rice vinegar
⅜ teaspoon sambal oelek (red chili paste)
1 tablespoon canola oil
¼ teaspoon kosher salt

GARLIC-THAI CHILE MIX
1 tablespoon minced fresh garlic
1½ teaspoons finely minced fresh Thai chile,
  with seeds

Prepare the Coriander Rub: Combine all the
ingredients and mix well. Leftover rub can
be stored in an airtight container at room
temperature.

Prepare the Thai Noodle Dressing: Place the
ginger, garlic, lemongrass and kaffir lime leaf in
a small food processor and blend thoroughly.

Add the sugar. Scrape down the sides and
process until the ingredients start to become
pasty. In a small bowl, whisk together the fish
sauce, vinegar, sambal oelek and canola oil.
Add the mixture from the food processor and
whisk to blend. Then whisk in the salt. Store,
covered, in the refrigerator, but let it come
to room temperature before use.

Prepare the Garlic-Thai Chile Mix: Combine
the ingredients until evenly blended.

To cook the noodles, immerse in boiling water
for 15 to 20 seconds, then immediately run
under cold water, drain, and let cool. Set aside
at room temperature.

To prepare the beef, season the meat with 2½
teaspoons of the rub. Then add the garlic-chile
mix, which is very spicy, so you may want to
wear gloves.

Using 2 large sauté pans, heat the olive oil over
high heat until just smoking. Add the seasoned
beef and sear, approximately 1½ to 2 minutes
on each side. Add the lime juice to the pan and
remove from the heat.

Place some noodles in the center of each plate,
mounding high. Surround the noodles with the
beef medallions.

Drizzle the dressing on the beef and noodles.
Sprinkle with the grapes. Garnish with
a cilantro sprig on top.

Note: The recipe calls for you to use 2 large sauté pans,
which ensures that the meat is not crowded and so will
brown quickly. If this is not possible, cook only half of the
meat at a time, and keep the seared meat warm while you
prepare the second batch. The caramelization or searing
of the meat is important to the flavor profile of this dish.

WINE:

The "life is too short" pick:

Müller-Catoir, Riesling, Spätlese, Pfalz, Germany 2007

The "just because it's inexpensive doesn't mean you're cheap" pick:

St. Urbans-Hof, Riesling, QbA, Mosel, Germany 2009

Alternatives: *A wine with a bit of residual sugar to balance the heat of the dish. Try a Moscato d'Asti or Brachetto d'Acqui from Italy.*

CEDAR PLANK ROASTED MUSHROOMS
SERVES 4

1 cup portobello mushrooms cut into 1½- to 2-inch chunks (it's okay to use some stems)
1 cup halved cremini mushrooms (stems okay)
½ cup shiitake mushrooms cut into 2- to 2½-inch pieces, stems removed (or other seasonal wild
    mushrooms)
1 tablespoon fresh lemon juice
6 tablespoons olive oil
½ teaspoon minced fresh garlic
1½ teaspoons Porcini Mushroom Rub (see note)
¼ teaspoon kosher or sea salt
⅛ teaspoon freshly ground black pepper
1 teaspoon chopped fresh thyme
¼ teaspoon chopped fresh rosemary
¼ teaspoon chopped fresh sage
1 half-moon lemon slice, ½ inch thick
1 large sprig *each* of fresh sage, thyme and rosemary

Special equipment: large cedar baking plank (page 25)

Preheat the oven to 375°F.

In a salad bowl, combine the mushrooms, lemon juice, olive oil, garlic, rub, salt, pepper and chopped herbs. Toss until completely coated. Transfer to the cedar plank, spreading to cover 95 percent of the surface.

Place the plank in the oven and bake for 12 to 15 minutes, or until the edges of the mushrooms are golden. Garnish with the lemon slice and herb sprigs.

Note: Chef Howie's 3 Chefs in a Tub rub can be substituted (page 25).

PORCINI MUSHROOM RUB
MAKES 1½ CUPS

1 cup finely ground dried Italian porcini
    mushrooms
6 tablespoons kosher salt
1 tablespoon plus 1 teaspoon dried
    thyme leaves
2 tablespoons plus 2 teaspoons minced
    lemon zest
1 teaspoon ground white pepper

Combine all the ingredients in a food processor and grind into a fine powder. Store in an airtight container at room temperature for up to 3 months.

Note: This rub can also be used to season steak, chicken, seafood or pasta. It has many uses.

WINE:
The "life is too short" pick:
Beaux Frères, Pinot Noir, Willamette Valley, Oregon 2008
The "just because it's inexpensive doesn't mean you're cheap" pick:
Stoller, Pinot Noir, Willamette Valley, Oregon 2008
Alternatives: *A fruit-driven red with moderate tannin and earthy notes. Bourgogne Rouge from France or Barbera from Italy.*

COPPER RIVER SALMON CARPACCIO
SERVES 4

6 ounces block-cut Copper River salmon (sockeye or king), sliced paper thin (see note)
⅛ teaspoon sea salt
3 tablespoons sliced frisée (¼-by-½-inch slices)
3 tablespoons sliced arugula (¼-by-1-inch slices)
1 tablespoon plus 1½ teaspoons sliced red onion (¹⁄₁₆-by-½-inch slices)
1½ teaspoons Lemon-Thyme Vinaigrette (page 62)
2 tablespoons crumbled ricotta salata (salted dry ricotta cheese)
1 tablespoon capers
1 tablespoon Preserved Lemon Oil
Black pepper, 6 turns of the mill

PRESERVED LEMON OIL
MAKES ½ CUP

3 tablespoons seeded, chopped Preserved Meyer Lemon (½-inch pieces)
1 teaspoon fresh lemon juice
⅓ cup first-press vintage extra-virgin olive oil (Capezzana or similar high-quality oil)

Prepare the Preserved Lemon Oil: In a Vitamix or other blender, puree the preserved lemon and lemon juice. Then slowly drizzle in the olive oil, blending until emulsified. Refrigerate until needed. The leftover oil will keep, refrigerated in a covered container, for 2 months. It can also be used in salads, on grilled fish and in a shrimp salad.

Place the sliced salmon on 4 individual plates or a large platter, with each piece slightly overlapping the previous piece. Season with the sea salt.

In a bowl, combine the frisée, arugula and red onion. Add the vinaigrette and toss until coated. Mound in the center of the plates or the platter.

Evenly distribute the ricotta, capers and preserved lemon oil over the salmon. Then evenly distribute the ground pepper.

Note: The salmon should be cut into a block portion, skin off, cleaned of any blood line. Freeze the block before slicing. Cut very thin, using a meat slicer.

WINE:
The "life is too short" pick:
Buty, Semillon-Sauvignon Blanc, Columbia Valley, Washington 2010
The "just because it's inexpensive doesn't mean you're cheap" pick:
Amavi, Semillon, Walla Walla Valley, Washington 2009
Alternatives: *A zippy white with citrus notes and a bit of richness. Bordeaux Blanc or rich Pinot Gris (Grigio).*

PRESERVED MEYER LEMONS

4 cups washed Meyer lemons cut into eighths
1 cup kosher salt
¼ cup sugar
1 cup fresh lemon juice

Place the lemons in a large bowl. Toss with the salt and sugar until completely coated.

Transfer to a glass jar with a glass lid.

Place in the refrigerator for 3 days (72 hours).

Then add the lemon juice and stir. Make sure the lemons are completely covered with the juice. Let the lemons sit at room temperature for 10 to 12 days, stirring every 2 days.

Refrigerate after the preserving is completed.

Rinse the lemons before using.

Note: Preserved lemons will keep for a year if refrigerated properly after curing. Store in a Kerr glass jar, sealed tightly.

PESTO CHICKEN ARANCINI (RISOTTO BALLS)
SERVES 4

ARANCINI RISOTTO BASE
2 tablespoons olive oil
1 teaspoon finely minced fresh garlic
2 teaspoons minced shallots
1¼ cups Arborio rice
¾ cup Chablis or similar white wine
3 cups Chicken Stock (page 120)

PESTO CHICKEN
½ pound boneless, skinless chicken breast
½ teaspoon salt, divided
¼ teaspoon ground black pepper
1 teaspoon olive oil
¼ cup Basil Pesto (page 29)

ARANCINI
1 tablespoon plus 1½ teaspoons sliced fresh chives (⅛-inch pieces)
2 cups panko bread crumbs
Canola oil, for deep-frying

For serving:

½ cup frisée cut into 1-inch pieces
½ cup baby arugula
2 tablespoons Garlic Aioli (page 84)
2 tablespoons pine nuts, toasted (page 73)
4 fresh basil sprigs

Special equipment: deep fryer

Notes: Additional broth may be needed during the final cooking stage of the risotto base to achieve the desired consistency. If you wind up with a little extra risotto base, you can use it to make risotto — just add more stock, and cheese.

Prepare the Arancini Risotto Base: Heat the olive oil in a heavy-gauge saucepan over medium-high heat. Add the garlic, shallots and rice. Stir to coat the rice and continue to sauté until the rice is pearlized (approximately 1 to 2 minutes). Add the wine and let reduce until the liquid is almost gone.

Add a quarter of the chicken stock. Lower the heat to medium, bring to a simmer, and let reduce, working the ingredients with a rubber spatula, until the liquid is almost gone. Add the remaining chicken stock ¼ cup at a time and continue to work and reduce until the rice is al dente and has a creamy medium-thick consistency. Transfer to a sheet pan, spread out evenly, and cool quickly in the refrigerator.

Prepare the Pesto Chicken:

Preheat the grill to medium-high.

Season the chicken with ¼ teaspoon salt and the pepper. Brush lightly with some of the olive oil. Grill for 2 minutes, then brush with olive oil, turn over, and cook until the internal temperature is 140°F. Remove from the grill and let cool.

When the chicken is completely cool, cut it into ¼-inch pieces. Mix with the pesto and ¼ teaspoon salt. Refrigerate until needed.

Note: The chicken can be cooked ahead of time and kept in the refrigerator, but once the pesto has been added, it should be used within an hour.

Prepare the Arancini: Mix the chives into the risotto base and make twenty 1-ounce loose risotto balls. Insert 1 tablespoon of the pesto chicken into the center of each ball. Re-form the balls around the chicken and roll in the panko until completely coated. Refrigerate until needed.

Heat the oil in a deep fryer according to the manufacturer's instructions. Add the risotto balls and cook for 2 to 3 minutes, or until golden brown and heated through. Remove from the fryer, place on paper towels to remove excess oil, and let rest for 30 seconds.

To serve, mix together the frisée and arugula. Place in a high mound on a serving plate.

Place the risotto balls on top of the greens, arranging evenly around the plate. Drizzle the greens and arancini with the aioli. Scatter the pine nuts over all. Garnish with basil sprigs.

WINE:
The "life is too short" pick:
Casa d'Ambra, Biancolella, Campania, Italy 2009
The "just because it's inexpensive doesn't mean you're cheap" pick:
Feudi di San Gregorio, Greco del Tufo, Campania, Italy 2009
Alternatives: *A dry white wine with some acidic zip and a round, opulent fruit edge. Albariño from Spain or California Sauvignon Blanc.*

WINE:

The "life is too short" pick:

Duval-Leroy, "Femme," Vertus, France 2006

The "just because it's inexpensive doesn't mean you're cheap" pick:

Roederer Estate, Brut, Anderson Valley, California

Alternatives: *A rich sparkling wine to balance the opulence of the dish. California sparkling wine or Prosecco.*

DEVILED EGGS WITH AHI TARTARE
SERVES 4

12 large eggs, hard-boiled for 8 minutes, peeled and sliced in half lengthwise
¾ cup Best Foods mayonnaise
⅛ teaspoon cayenne pepper
½ teaspoon granulated onion
1 teaspoon Colman's dry mustard
1 teaspoon wasabi paste or reconstituted dry
¾ cup Daikon-Carrot Mix
8 chive spears (2- to 3-inch diagonal slices)

ROASTED ONION
½ sweet white onion, peeled
½ teaspoon canola oil

AHI TARTARE
⅓ cup diced ahi tuna (⅛- to ³⁄₁₆-inch pieces)
1 teaspoon diced medium-crisp cooked bacon (⅛-inch pieces)
1 teaspoon minced Roasted Onion
½ teaspoon sliced chives (¹⁄₁₆-inch pieces)
1½ teaspoons Black Truffle Vinaigrette (page 63)

Special equipment: pastry bag with a medium-size star tip

Prepare the Roasted Onion: Preheat the oven broiler. Remove 3 to 4 layers of the onion. Coat with the oil and place on a sheet pan. Roast under the broiler until golden brown. Let cool, then mince into ⅛-inch pieces. Refrigerate until needed.

To prepare the eggs, combine the egg yolks and mayonnaise in a mixing bowl. With a whisk attachment or regular beaters, whip until creamy. Blend in the cayenne, granulated onion, mustard and wasabi. Transfer to the pastry bag and pipe into the egg white halves. Refrigerate until needed.

Prepare the Ahi Tartare:

Combine the ahi, bacon, roasted onion, chives and vinaigrette in a bowl and toss until well blended. Place equal amounts of the mixture on top of the deviled eggs.

To serve, place the daikon-carrot mix on a platter, arrange the eggs on top, and garnish with the chive spears.

DAIKON-CARROT MIX

1 large daikon radish,
            12 ounces peeled weight
1 medium carrot,
            4 ounces peeled weight

Peel the daikon and carrot. Hand-shred them with a Japanese mandoline, using the fine shredding plate, into 3- to 4-inch by ¹⁄₁₆-inch pieces. This can also be done by hand if you have good knife skills and a very sharp knife. Cut the daikon into 3-inch-long rectangles, then ¹⁄₁₆-inch-thick slices, and then ¹⁄₁₆-inch-thick strands. Do the same with the carrot.

Soak the shredded daikon and carrot in cold water for 20 minutes. Then rinse and strain. Store in the refrigerator until ready to use.

One thing I did learn from John is striving for excellence on a daily basis. His manner can be intimidating, but that is just how he is. People will say, "You know John's here." I do the same thing whether he is here or not; I'm always doing what he expects. This work ethic is what I've learned from John: You do the right thing regardless of what it is, when it is. If you see something wrong, fix it. Look for a solution. It has to be perfect all the time. What we learn are life lessons, making it better, making ourselves better. And I take these lessons with me when I go home. It is a constant work in progress.

STEVE COBLE
CHEF
SEASTAR RESTAURANT & RAW BAR

It's the finer details, looking at how the restaurants look, how we look. All of us are representative of Seastar, which means we represent John, because this is his restaurant. But as managers, we have ownership, so it represents us, too. When I get dressed in the morning, how do I want to look? What do we want people to think of Seastar? We want it represented well. This is something that John has taught us. We are not just a restaurant; this is our family, and look at what we have accomplished. It makes you want to do better. If you see somebody do something incorrect, you let them know this is not what we do. Everybody holds everybody accountable. We are at the same level and we have pride — he has made sure of that. He could not have done this alone; we all had a part.

KAREY COBLE
MANAGER / PARTNER
SEASTAR RESTAURANT & RAW BAR

CEVICHE

MAHI MAHI CEVICHE WITH PINEAPPLE AND SWEET ONION
SERVES 4

2 tablespoons fresh lime juice
2 tablespoons fresh lemon juice
4 tablespoons fresh orange juice
2 tablespoons pineapple juice
1 teaspoon turbinado sugar (raw sugar)
¼ teaspoon sea salt
¼ teaspoon coarsely ground black pepper
1½ cups (12 ounces) fresh mahi mahi pieces, blood line removed
      (½- to ¾-inch pieces)
4 coconut shells (or martini glasses)
2 tablespoons unsweetened shaved coconut, toasted
4 fresh cilantro sprigs

Note: Other varieties of white fish can be used for this dish, including ono, halibut, marlin and Gulf snapper. The fish must marinate — "cook" — for at least 5 hours in order for the acids in the lime and lemon juice to perform the cooking action.

PINEAPPLE RELISH
6 tablespoons sliced sweet white onion (¹⁄₁₆-by-1-inch pieces)
¾ cup diced fresh pineapple (⅛-inch pieces)
¼ cup tangelo, tangerine or satsuma pieces, membrane removed
      (¼-inch pieces)
1½ teaspoons very finely minced seeded fresh red jalapeño
2 teaspoons fresh lime juice
1 tablespoon coarsely chopped fresh cilantro
½ teaspoon crushed toasted coriander
½ teaspoon sea salt
2 teaspoons olive oil

In a bowl, combine the juices, sugar, salt and pepper, stirring to blend. Add the mahi mahi and marinate in the refrigerator for at least 5 hours and up to 8 hours.

Drain the fish and refrigerate until needed.

Prepare the Pineapple Relish: Combine all the ingredients and stir until well blended. Refrigerate until needed.

To serve, mix the mahi mahi ceviche with the pineapple relish and spoon into the coconut shells. Top with the toasted coconut and garnish with the cilantro sprigs.

WINE:
    Mantel Blanco, Verdejo, Rueda, Spain 2009
    Alternatives: *Super-high-acid wine with some tropical fruit notes. New Zealand Sauvignon Blanc.*

With any ceviche, it is important to recognize the acid that is used to "cook" the fish. The wine must have as much acidity as or more than the dish to make a balanced match.

CALIFORNIA YELLOWTAIL JACK CEVICHE
SERVES 4

8 ounces California yellowtail jack (hamachi), very thinly sliced
    (about 24 slices)
Black pepper
2 tablespoons thinly sliced red onion (1 inch long by $\frac{1}{16}$ inch thick)
4 teaspoons coarsely chopped fresh cilantro, plus 4 sprigs for garnish
16 orange segments, membrane removed
16 slices ($\frac{3}{16}$ inch) green olive stuffed with pimiento

CEVICHE MARINADE
2 tablespoons fresh lime juice
$\frac{3}{8}$ teaspoon freshly ground black pepper
1 tablespoon plus 2 teaspoons olive oil
$\frac{1}{4}$ teaspoon sugar
$\frac{3}{8}$ teaspoon seeded and very finely minced habanero chile

There are several different styles of ceviche — from South American to Caribbean to Spanish. Each ethnic area has unique flavor profiles that are added to their dishes, and the different versions show the cultural variations.

To prepare the marinade, combine all the ingredients. Mix well until the sugar is dissolved. Transfer to a squeeze bottle and refrigerate until needed.

On each of 4 plates, line the slices of fish from one end of the plate to the other, slightly overlapping if necessary. Sprinkle black pepper over the fish, using 2 turns of the pepper mill for each plate.

Next, drizzle the fish evenly with the marinade.

Sprinkle the fish with the red onions and chopped cilantro.

Neatly arrange the orange segments, evenly spaced, on top of the fish. Place the olives next to the oranges. Garnish each plate with a cilantro sprig.

WINE:
Jaume Serra, "Cristalino," Cava, Spain
Alternatives: *Look for a sparkling wine with bracing acidity. Prosecco from Italy.*

With any ceviche, it is important to recognize the acid that is used to "cook" the fish. The wine must have as much acidity as or more than the dish to make a balanced match.

HALIBUT CEVICHE WITH ROASTED CORN AND AVOCADO
SERVES 4

3 tablespoons fresh lime juice

6 tablespoons fresh lemon juice

2 tablespoons tomato juice

½ teaspoon sea salt

½ teaspoon coarsely ground black pepper

2 cups (1 pound) diced skinless halibut, blood line removed (½- to ¾-inch pieces)

¾ teaspoon Tabasco sauce

4 fresh cilantro sprigs

ROASTED CORN
1 ear of corn

1 teaspoon olive oil

¼ teaspoon sea salt

ROASTED CORN AVOCADO RELISH
¼ cup diced white onion (⅛-inch pieces)

½ cup diced seeded Roma tomato (¼-inch pieces)

3 tablespoons diced ripe tomatillo (¼-inch pieces)

¾ teaspoon minced seeded fresh jalapeño

1½ teaspoons fresh lime juice

1 tablespoon coarsely chopped fresh cilantro

⅜ teaspoon sea salt

¼ cup olive oil

½ cup roasted corn kernels

¼ cup diced firm ripe avocado (½-inch pieces)

TORTILLA STRIPS
Canola oil, for deep-frying

¾ pound 6-inch corn tortillas

1½ teaspoons sea salt

Special equipment: deep fryer

WINE:
Santiago Ruiz, Rias Baixas, Spain 2009
Alternatives: *A high-acid wine with some ripe fruit richness. Verdejo from Spain or Chenin Blanc (Vouvray or Montlouis) from France.*

In a nonreactive container, mix the juices, salt and pepper. Add the halibut and marinate in the refrigerator for at least 5 hours and up to 8 hours. Drain the halibut completely and refrigerate until needed.

Prepare the Roasted Corn: Remove the husk and silk from the corn. Brush the ear with the olive oil, then season with salt.

Roast over medium-high heat on an outdoor grill or in a grill pan, or over an open flame, for about 2½ to 3 minutes, making a quarter turn every 30 seconds or so, until the corn is golden brown and slightly charred. Some of the kernels should be caramelized through the skin, and some will be slightly charred. Let cool, then cut the kernels off the cob. Refrigerate until needed.

Prepare the Roasted Corn Avocado Relish: Combine all the ingredients except the corn and avocado. Mix until well coated. Add the roasted corn and toss well, then lightly fold in the avocado.

Prepare the Tortilla Strips: Heat the oil in the deep fryer to 375°F.

Cut each tortilla into four 1½-inch strips. Place in the fryer and cook until golden brown, about 30 seconds. Remove from the oil and let drain on paper towels. Season the strips with the salt. Keep, covered, at room temperature until needed.

To serve, combine the roasted corn avocado relish with the halibut ceviche and Tabasco sauce. Lightly toss until well mixed. Divide evenly among 4 small bowls and garnish with the cilantro sprigs. Place each bowl on a plate and surround the bowl with the tortilla strips.

SCALLOP CEVICHE WITH MANGO-KIWI RELISH
SERVES 4

3 tablespoons fresh lime juice

5 tablespoons fresh Meyer lemon juice

⅛ teaspoon sea salt

¼ teaspoon coarsely ground black pepper

10 fresh sea scallops (10/20 count), preferably smaller scallops (¾ to 1 ounce each), side muscles removed, sliced in half

8 cups crushed ice

20 singing pink sea scallop shells, cleaned (see note)

4 lime slices – ½-inch-thick quarter slices

4 fresh cilantro sprigs

Note: If you don't have scallop shells, use plates, arranging the scallops slightly overlapping and leaving a hole in the center for the relish.

MANGO-KIWI RELISH
MAKES ¾ CUP

6 tablespoons diced firm fresh mango (¼-inch pieces)

3 tablespoons diced fresh kiwi (¼-inch pieces)

½ teaspoon very finely grated fresh orange zest

2 teaspoons fresh lime juice

2 tablespoons minced sweet Maui or white onion (⅛-inch pieces)

1 tablespoon diced red bell pepper (⅛-inch pieces)

⅛ teaspoon very finely minced habanero chile

⅛ teaspoon very finely minced jalapeño chile

1 tablespoon fresh orange juice

1 teaspoon thinly sliced fresh cilantro

In a nonreactive container, mix together the lime and lemon juice, salt and pepper. Drain the scallops well and add to the mixture. Marinate in the refrigerator for at least 3 hours and up to 5 hours. (The scallops must be marinated for at least 3 hours in order for the acids in the citrus juice to perform the cooking action.) Drain the scallops and refrigerate until needed.

Prepare the Mango-Kiwi Relish: Combine all the ingredients and toss until well coated. Refrigerate until needed.

To serve, place the crushed ice on 4 deep plates or bowls. Place the scallop slices on the shells. Top each scallop with 1½ teaspoons of mango-kiwi relish, being sure to toss the relish often to keep the juices evenly distributed. Place 5 filled scallop shells on each plate, making sure that they sit flat so the juices don't drip off. Garnish with the lime slices and cilantro sprigs.

WINE:
Henri Bourgeois, Quincy (Sauvignon Blanc), Loire, France 2010
Alternatives: *Super-high-acid wine with some tropical fruit richness and citrus zip. New Zealand Sauvignon Blanc.*

John called a few of us into the office and told us he was leaving Palisade. I was shocked. Palisade was John Howie. He was the central person. When he walked around, everybody tightened up, everyone wanted to be perfect, front of the house, servers, everyone. Terrance, a chef, was chosen to go, and he told me he had spoken to John about me. So John took all the sous-chefs out to dinner one night, to a restaurant in Seattle. That night he told me about his vision of Seastar. He was doing all the work, design, plates ... and he was really excited to share it. That sort of energy got me excited. He offered ownership to all the managers. I was going to be part of growing something. We just knew John would succeed.

Even at Palisade, the idea and the goal was always to hire the best. We care and that's one of the rules we live by. Whenever we need someone, we look at the inside first. One of our lead cooks was the third cook hired, and started as pantry cook, really worked hard and worked up — it's so important. We will not compromise on quality. We can compromise on speed because we can get you an extra hand, but not quality. That integrity is something that has to be first and foremost. We give everybody a ruler, measuring spoons — this is what they are issued as part of the uniform. The recipe will say celery, ¼-inch diced, and we measure. That is how detailed those recipes are.

JOE HAYNES
CHEF / PARTNER
SEASTAR RESTAURANT & RAW BAR

DRESSINGS

LEMON-CHIVE OIL
MAKES ¼ CUP

3 tablespoons fresh chives cut into ½-inch
        pieces
¼ cup extra-virgin olive oil
¾ teaspoon minced fresh lemon zest
1½ teaspoons fresh lemon juice

Immerse the chives in boiling water for
10 seconds, then immediately cool under
cold water. Drain well.

Combine all the ingredients in a small blender
and process until completely pureed. Strain
through a fine-mesh strainer lined with
cheesecloth, transfer to a squeeze bottle,
and refrigerate until needed.

RASPBERRY VINAIGRETTE
MAKES 2 CUPS

½ cup raspberry red wine vinegar
7 tablespoons sugar
1½ teaspoons kosher salt
1 teaspoon coarsely ground black pepper
1 tablespoon very finely minced shallots
⅞ cup canola oil

In an electric mixer, combine the vinegar,
sugar, salt, pepper and shallots. Mix until the
sugar is dissolved.

Drizzle in the canola oil very slowly, mixing
until well blended.

Refrigerate in an airtight container for up to
3 months.

Stir well before using.

LEMON-THYME VINAIGRETTE
MAKES 1 CUP

2 tablespoons very finely minced white onion
¾ teaspoon minced fresh garlic
¼ cup white wine vinegar
1 tablespoon Dijon mustard
2 tablespoons fresh lemon juice
1 teaspoon minced fresh lemon zest
½ teaspoon minced fresh thyme
½ teaspoon coarsely ground black pepper
¾ teaspoon sea salt
½ cup olive oil

In a bowl, combine all ingredients except the
olive oil, stirring until the salt is dissolved.
Slowly whisk in the oil.

Refrigerate, covered, until needed.

BLACK TRUFFLE VINAIGRETTE

YIELD: ½ CUP
¼ cup red wine vinegar
1 tablespoon hand-minced shallot (¹⁄₁₆-inch pieces)
1 teaspoon fresh lemon juice
2 teaspoons hand-minced black truffle (¹⁄₁₆-inch pieces)
¼ teaspoon sea salt
⅛ teaspoon freshly ground black pepper
2 tablespoons extra-virgin olive oil
2 tablespoons white truffle oil (my favorite
      is Tartufare)

YIELD: 2 CUPS
1 cup red wine vinegar
¼ cup hand-minced shallots (¹⁄₁₆-inch pieces)
1 tablespoon plus 1 teaspoon fresh lemon juice
2 tablespoons plus 2 teaspoons hand-minced black truffle (¹⁄₁₆-inch pieces)
1 teaspoon sea salt
½ teaspoon freshly ground black pepper
½ cup extra-virgin olive oil
½ cup white truffle oil (my favorite is Tartufare)

Combine all ingredients except the oils and mix until well blended. Then slowly whisk in the oils.

Store, covered, in the refrigerator for up to one month.

Note: One of our recipe testers asked me to include a recipe for white-truffle-infused olive oil. I could do that, but the cost of white truffles is astronomical in comparison to that of black truffles. It is better to just purchase a white-truffle-infused olive oil.

MAYTAG BLUE CHEESE DRESSING
MAKES 2 CUPS

½ teaspoon very finely minced fresh garlic

1½ teaspoons very finely minced sweet onion

2 tablespoons red wine vinegar

¼ teaspoon Worcestershire sauce

6 tablespoons sour cream

1 cup mayonnaise

¼ cup buttermilk

¼ teaspoon dry mustard (I prefer Colman's)

¼ teaspoon coarsely ground black pepper

½ teaspoon granulated onion

A pinch of ground white pepper

6 tablespoons Maytag blue cheese
      (¼-inch chunks)

In a large mixing bowl with a paddle attachment, combine the garlic, onion, vinegar, Worcestershire sauce, sour cream, mayonnaise and buttermilk. Mix on low speed for 1 to 2 minutes.

Add the dry mustard, black pepper, granulated onion and white pepper. Mix for 1 minute.

Add the cheese and blend for 1 to 2 minutes.

Refrigerate, covered, for 24 hours to let the flavors blend. This will keep for up to 2 weeks in the refrigerator in an airtight container.

Note: This recipe calls for Maytag blue cheese. Yes, it is the same people who make the washers and dryers. They have a small dairy farm in Iowa that produces the best blue cheese. Maytag is a very creamy, mild blue cheese. You can use another blue cheese that has similar qualities. A sharper cheese may not have the desired result.

BLUE CHEESE VINAIGRETTE
MAKES 2 CUPS

½ cup red wine vinegar

2 tablespoons fresh lemon juice

1 tablespoon Dijon mustard

½ teaspoon finely minced fresh garlic

2 teaspoons kosher salt

1 teaspoon freshly ground black pepper

1 cup olive oil

¼ cup crumbled blue cheese

In an electric mixer, combine the vinegar, lemon juice, mustard, garlic, salt and pepper. Mix until the salt is dissolved. Then drizzle in the olive oil very slowly, mixing until well blended and emulsified.

Remove from the mixer and fold in the blue cheese.

Refrigerate in an airtight container for up to a month. Stir well before using.

CAESAR DRESSING
MAKES 2 CUPS

⅜ cup egg yolks
3 tablespoons anchovies
1 tablespoon very finely minced fresh garlic
¾ teaspoon coarsely ground black pepper
1 tablespoon plus 1½ teaspoons red wine
    vinegar
3 tablespoons fresh lemon juice
2¼ teaspoons Dijon mustard
1 teaspoon Worcestershire sauce
¼ teaspoon Tabasco sauce
1 teaspoon sea salt
1 cup olive oil

Place the egg yolks in a mixer with a wire whip attachment. Whip on medium-high speed until the yolks begin to thicken and turn light yellow.

Place the anchovies and garlic in a mini food processor and process until the anchovies are pureed. Add to the egg yolks and mix well.

One at a time, add the pepper, vinegar, lemon juice, mustard, Worcestershire sauce, Tabasco sauce and salt, mixing on medium speed after each addition until well blended.

Increase the speed to medium-high and slowly drizzle in the olive oil. Continue to mix until the dressing is emulsified.

Refrigerate in an airtight container for up to a month.

TOMATO-THYME DRESSING
MAKES 1 CUP

1 tablespoon fresh white or sweet onion juice
    (see note)
3 tablespoons double-concentrate tomato paste
¼ cup peeled, seeded and diced Roma tomato
    (¼-inch pieces)
¼ cup white balsamic vinegar
2 tablespoons plus 1½ teaspoons sugar
¾ teaspoon chopped fresh thyme leaves
¼ teaspoon freshly ground black pepper
³⁄₁₆ teaspoon freshly ground white pepper
½ cup olive oil

Place all ingredients except the olive oil in a blender and puree. Then slowly drizzle in the oil.

Refrigerate in a covered container for at least 12 hours to let the flavors blend. Stir thoroughly before using.

Note: To make the onion juice, you will need ¼ cup of onions that have been finely minced in a mini food processor. Place the onions on a piece of cheesecloth and squeeze out the liquid.

All the people who are now a part of our team here have been associated with John for a minimum of 7 years and many for 20 years. John spends time with each of his restaurants. I don't know how he does it. We have weekly meetings here, and he devotes the same amount of time to each restaurant. He cares so much about each one.

He's very intense when it comes to the restaurant and taking care of guests. But he's there to help everybody. He's a gentle giant. He can be very stern and strict in the restaurant. He has very high expectations for everything that goes on in all his restaurants, and he holds people accountable. He's probably one of the hardest-working restaurateurs I've ever met. He's constantly working and somehow he manages, with his son JoJo and all the other commitments. As a team we have that same care level and that's really what it boils down to. When we've had a successful year, we have bonus programs. We all have ownership in the restaurant, so it's just like being investors. When there is a profit margin, we get a portion. It's not just a job, it's ownership that we have.

He is the epitome of leading by example. John cares about people. In general it doesn't matter who they are. He is one of the most caring and giving people I have ever met. He has been blessed with a talent, and everything he gets from that talent he shares.

MARK MANCA
CHILDHOOD FRIEND
RESTAURANT PARTNER

SALADS, SAUCES & SIDES

DUNGENESS CRAB SALAD WITH AVOCADO AND GRAPEFRUIT

SERVES 4

¾ cup (6 to 8 ounces) fresh Dungeness crab meat (see note)
1 tablespoon plus 1½ teaspoons very finely minced celery
1 tablespoon very finely minced sweet white onion
1½ teaspoons sliced fresh chives (⅛-inch pieces)
3 tablespoons diced firm but tender avocado (⅛-inch pieces)
12 red or pink grapefruit sections, membrane removed
8 lengthwise slices of avocado, ¼ inch thick
2 tablespoons Tomato-Thyme Dressing (page 65)
¼ cup micro peppercress or micro greens (see note)

Note: Crab should be used within 24 hours of purchase.

Note: If micro peppercress or micro greens are not available, pick out some small watercress to use as a substitute.

CREAMY LEMON CHIVE DRESSING
2 tablespoons Best Foods mayonnaise
½ teaspoon very, very finely minced lemon zest
½ teaspoon fresh lemon juice
¾ teaspoon very thinly sliced chives
Pinch of ground white pepper
⅛ teaspoon sea salt – flake, not coarse-grind

Special equipment: 2-inch-diameter, 2-inch-high plastic ring; squeeze bottle

Prepare the Creamy Lemon Chive Dressing: In a bowl, combine all the ingredients and mix until completely incorporated. Cover and refrigerate for at least 2 hours to let the flavors blend. Stir thoroughly before using.

To prepare the salad, mix the crab, celery, onion and chives together in a bowl. Gently fold in the dressing, taking care not to break up all the crab. Fold in the diced avocado. Refrigerate until needed.

For each serving, place the plastic ring in the center of a plate. Fill the ring with a quarter of the crab salad. Lightly press the salad down into the ring and then pull the ring off. Place the grapefruit and avocado slices on the right side of the crab salad, fanned toward the bottom of the plate, alternating grapefruit with avocado.

Next, put the tomato-thyme dressing in a squeeze bottle. Start with a large drop of dressing on the upper-left side of each plate and then work down toward the bottom, placing 4 more increasingly smaller drops. Top each crabmeat tower with micro cress or greens.

WINE:
The "life is too short" pick:
Edmond Vatan, Clos la Néore, Sancerre, Loire, France 2007
The "just because it's inexpensive doesn't mean you're cheap" pick:
Domaine Henry Pellé, Menetou-Salon, Loire, France 2010
Alternatives: *A fresh and lively white wine with citrus notes that balances the delicacy of the crab and the richness of the avocado. A Dry Sauvignon Blanc or Pinot Gris (Grigio).*

THAI SEAFOOD SALAD
SERVES 4

⅜ cup tako (cooked octopus) sliced in 1/16-inch rounds (see note)
1 cup cooked bay shrimp
¾ cup sliced Maui sweet onion (quartered, then cut in ⅛-inch slices)
2 tablespoons very, very thinly sliced fresh mint
1½ teaspoons very, very thinly sliced fresh kaffir lime leaf
3 tablespoons coarsely chopped fresh cilantro
¼ cup chopped peanuts (¼-inch pieces), lightly toasted
4 Napa cabbage leaves
4 large fresh mint sprigs
4 lime wedges, ½ inch thick

Note: Tako (sushi-grade octopus) is very expensive. You could substitute blanched calamari legs and tentacles. Cook them the same way you would cook the calamari rings.

SRIRACHA DRESSING
6 tablespoons fresh lime juice
¼ cup sugar
2 tablespoons finely minced lemongrass (1/16-inch pieces), tender inner stalk only
1 tablespoon plus 1 teaspoon Sriracha red chili sauce (preferably Shark brand)
2 tablespoons Thai fish sauce
½ teaspoon minced Thai chile, with seeds

BLANCHED CALAMARI RINGS
1 teaspoon kosher salt
2 quarts water
¾ cup calamari cut into ¼-inch rings

Prepare the Sriracha Dressing: Combine all the ingredients and mix until blended. Store, covered, in the refrigerator until needed.

Prepare the Blanched Calamari Rings: Salt the water and bring to a boil. Place the calamari in the water and blanch for 30 seconds — no longer or they will be rubbery and tough. Remove from the water and run under cold water for 60 seconds, until slightly cooled. Place in the refrigerator and let cool completely.

To prepare the salad, combine the calamari, tako, shrimp, onions, herbs and peanuts in a small bowl. Add the dressing and toss until completely coated. Let sit for 30 seconds so the seafood and onions can absorb the flavors of the dressing.

Place a cabbage leaf on each plate. Toss the salad again and place on top of the cabbage leaves, mounded high. Don't pour the dressing remaining in the bowl over the top. Garnish with a mint sprig in the center of the mound, with a lime wedge next to it.

WINE:
The "life is too short" pick:
Robert Weil, Riesling, Spätlese, Rheingau, Germany 2007
The "just because it's inexpensive doesn't mean you're cheap" pick:
Efeste, Riesling, "Evergreen Vineyard," Columbia Valley, Washington 2009
Alternatives: *An off-dry (semi-sweet) white wine to balance the heat of the dish. Fruity Oregon Pinot Gris or California Gewürztraminer.*

BLUE CHEESE, SHRIMP AND PEAR SALAD
SERVES 4

3 cups julienne-sliced romaine lettuce hearts (¾-inch slices)
1 cup julienne-sliced curly endive (½-inch slices)
1 cup Maytag Blue Cheese Dressing (page 64)
¼ cup hazelnuts, toasted
½ cup cooked bay shrimp
½ cup Sweet 100 tomatoes
¼ cup blue cheese crumbles
1 cup julienne-sliced crisp unpeeled pear
      (⅛ by ⅛ by 1 to 2 inches) – do not slice
      until ready to serve

GRILLED RADICCHIO-BELGIAN ENDIVE MIX
½ very small head radicchio (cut lengthwise)
½ very small head Belgian endive (cut lengthwise)
1 tablespoon olive oil

Prepare the Radicchio–Belgian Endive Mix: Preheat the grill or a grill pan to high.

Be sure to grill the radicchio and endive heads intact, otherwise the leaves will become too soft. Baste with the olive oil. Place on a very hot grill or grill pan and grill on both sides just until grill marks appear. Don't let it get soft. Cool in the refrigerator until completely chilled.

Cut the radicchio into 1- to 2-inch by ¼-inch slices. Cut the endive crosswise into ¼-inch slices. Toss together and refrigerate until needed.

To prepare the salad, combine the romaine, endive and grilled mix in a large bowl. Add the dressing and toss until completely coated. Place on plates or a platter and top with the hazelnuts, shrimp, tomatoes and blue cheese crumbles. Slice the pear and place on top of the salad. Be sure to serve immediately, as the pear will brown quickly once it is sliced.

Notes: Any remaining fresh endive or radicchio can be cut up and used in a salad mix. The julienned pear is easily prepared on a French or Japanese mandoline.

HOW TO TOAST NUTS

Nuts are best toasted at lower temperatures. This allows some room for error. The nuts should be tossed and turned often. Once they are toasted to the desired color, the nuts should be removed from the hot pan, as they will continue to toast.

Preheat the oven to 275°F. Place the nuts on a sheet pan, spreading evenly in a single layer. Don't mound them, or they may not cook evenly.

Place in the oven and toast, stirring every 5 minutes. Watch the nuts carefully — they should be golden in color and not too dark, or they will have a bitter taste.

Remove from the oven and let cool on a rack to room temperature. Store in an airtight container at room temperature.

WINE:
The "life is too short" pick:
Camille Savès, "Carte Blanche," Bouzy, Champagne, France
The "just because it's inexpensive doesn't mean you're cheap" pick:
Argyle, Brut, Willamette Valley, Oregon 2009
Alternatives: *A rich sparkling wine. Italian Prosecco or German Sekt.*

Spinach Salad with Strawberries and Enoki Mushrooms
Serves 4

6 cups (about ½ pound) baby spinach, stems removed
½ cup julienne-sliced sweet onion (⅛-by-1-inch slices)
1½ cups (about ¾ pound) sliced strawberries (¼ inch thick)
1 package (2 ounces) enoki mushrooms, separated into long strips (see note)
4 tablespoons Candied Five-Spice Cashews

Candied Five-Spice Cashews

1 egg white
1 tablespoon water
1 pound cashew pieces
⅓ cup sugar
1 tablespoon Chinese five-spice powder
½ teaspoon ground star anise
½ teaspoon kosher salt
½ teaspoon ground cayenne pepper

Honey-Sesame Dressing

¼ cup seasoned rice vinegar
2 tablespoons distilled white vinegar
2 tablespoons plus 1½ teaspoons sugar
2 tablespoons plus 1½ teaspoons honey
2¼ teaspoons coarsely ground black pepper
1 tablespoon plus 1½ teaspoons white sesame seeds, toasted golden brown
1½ teaspoons toasted sesame oil
½ cup canola oil

Prepare the Candied Five-Spice Cashews: Preheat the oven to 325°F.

In a stainless steel bowl, whip the egg white and water together
until foamy. Add the cashew pieces and toss to coat. Place the nuts
in a strainer and let drain for at least 2 minutes.

In a large, dry bowl mix the remaining ingredients. Add the nuts and toss until completely coated.

Spread the nuts out on a sheet pan in a single layer. Bake for 20 minutes. Reduce the oven temperature to 200°F. Stir the nuts and bake for another 15 to 20 minutes, or until dry. Let cool, then store in an airtight container at room temperature.

Prepare the Honey-Sesame Dressing: Place the vinegars, sugar, honey and pepper in a mixing bowl and blend until the sugar is dissolved.

Add the sesame seeds, then slowly drizzle in the sesame and canola oil, whisking to emulsify the dressing. Refrigerate until needed.

To assemble the salad, combine the spinach, onions, strawberries and three-quarters of the mushrooms in a salad bowl, and toss to blend. Stir the dressing well and add to the salad. Lightly toss until well coated.

Place the salad on 4 plates, mounded high. Be sure to bring some strawberries and mushrooms to the top. Sprinkle the remaining mushrooms on top of the salad. Garnish with the candied cashews.

Note: Enoki mushrooms are sold in one- to two-ounce packages and will be grown together — they must be pulled apart almost like string cheese.

WINE:
The "life is too short" pick:
Veuve Clicquot, Demi-Sec, Reims, France
The "just because it's inexpensive doesn't mean you're cheap" pick:
La Spinetta, Moscato d'Asti, Piedmont, Italy 2010
Alternatives: *An off-dry (semi-sweet) sparkling wine. Italian Brachetto.*

SEASONAL GREENS, PEACHES AND HARICOT VERT SALAD

SERVES 4

6 cups seasonal greens or baby spinach, or both
½ cup diagonally halved blanched haricot verts (al dente)
¼ cup julienne-sliced red onion (¹⁄₁₆ by 1 to 2 inches)
¾ cup sliced peeled peaches (⅛ inch thick)
¾ cup Sweet and Sour Mustard Dressing
¼ cup Candied Almonds

CANDIED ALMONDS

MAKES 1 CUP
¾ cup sugar
1 cup sliced raw almonds

Note: Other stone fruits such as nectarines, apricots, plums or even Rainier cherries can be used instead of or in addition to the peaches.

SWEET AND SOUR MUSTARD DRESSING

MAKES 1 CUP
¼ cup white wine vinegar
¼ cup whole-grain mustard
¼ cup sugar
½ teaspoon salt
½ teaspoon coarsely ground black pepper
¼ teaspoon Tabasco sauce
½ cup canola oil

Prepare the Candied Almonds: Heat the sugar and almonds in a nonstick sauté pan over medium-low heat until the sugar caramelizes and the almonds are toasted (some charring is okay).

Transfer the candied almonds to a sheet pan. With a wooden spoon, gently spread the almonds over the surface of the pan, avoiding breaking them. Use pan spray if needed to ease the spreading process. Let cool just enough to handle. Using your fingers, gently separate the sliced almonds into tiny clusters. When the almonds have completely cooled, store in an airtight container at room temperature.

Prepare the Sweet and Sour Mustard Dressing: In a mixer with a whip attachment, combine all the ingredients except the oil. Blend until the sugar is dissolved. Slowly drizzle in the oil, whipping until well mixed. Refrigerate until needed.

To assemble the salad, combine the greens, haricot verts, onions and peaches in a bowl. Add the dressing and toss to coat.

Mound the salad onto 4 chilled salad plates. Top with the candied almonds.

WINE:
The "life is too short" pick:
Guigal, Condrieu, Rhône, France 2009
The "just because it's inexpensive doesn't mean you're cheap" pick:
McCrea, Viognier, Yakima Valley, Washington 2009
Alternatives: *A rich white wine with stone-fruit notes. Alsatian Gewürztraminer or super-ripe Oregon Pinot Gris.*

SPINACH AND GOLDEN BEET SALAD WITH MAPLE VINAIGRETTE
SERVES 4

3 cups baby spinach, cleaned, stems removed
½ head of butter lettuce, soft outside leaves
    removed, cut into ½-inch slices
½ cup very thinly sliced cooked golden beet –
    1 large golden beet, boiled until tender,
    peeled, and sliced paper thin (see note)
¾ cup Maple Vinaigrette
¼ cup sweetened dried cranberries
⅜ cup crumbled blue cheese (¼-inch pieces)
¼ cup Candied Walnuts

PICKLED GRILLED RED ONIONS
⅓ cup sugar
⅓ cup distilled white vinegar
1 teaspoon kosher salt
4 slices red onion – medium-sized onion,
    peeled and cut horizontally into
    ¼-inch-thick rounds
¾ teaspoon olive oil
½ cup water

CANDIED WALNUTS
MAKES 2 CUPS
1 egg white
1 tablespoon water
2 cups walnuts, halves and quarters only
¾ cup sugar
1 teaspoon kosher salt

MAPLE VINAIGRETTE
MAKES 1 CUP
½ teaspoon very finely minced shallots
¼ teaspoon very finely minced fresh garlic
¼ cup pure maple syrup
3 tablespoons white balsamic vinegar
1 tablespoon plus 1 teaspoon fresh lemon juice
1½ teaspoons whole-grain mustard
⅛ teaspoon medium-ground black pepper
⅛ teaspoon sea salt
½ cup olive oil

Note: Beets can be sliced on a French or Japanese
mandoline to achieve the desired paper-thin appearance.

Prepare the Pickled Grilled Red Onions: In a saucepan, combine sugar, vinegar and salt. Bring to a boil over medium-high heat. Let cool. If not using immediately, transfer to a stainless steel or plastic container and refrigerate until needed.

Preheat the outdoor grill or a grill pan to medium-high.

Brush the onions with olive oil. Place them on the grill or grill pan and cook until grill marks have formed, then turn and cook the other side until grill marks have formed. Remove from the heat and place in a shallow nonreactive pan. Add the water to the vinegar mixture. Pour over the onions and marinate in the refrigerator for 3 hours, stirring occasionally to ensure uniform marination.

Remove the onions from the marinade and refrigerate until needed.

Prepare the Candied Walnuts: Preheat the oven to 250°F.

In a stainless steel bowl, whip the egg white and water together until foamy. Add the walnuts and toss to coat.

In a large, dry bowl combine the sugar and salt, and stir to blend. Add the nuts and toss until completely coated. Spread the nuts on a rimmed sheet pan in a single layer. Bake for 40 minutes, then reduce the heat to 200°F. Stir the nuts and bake for another 30 minutes, or until dry. Let cool to room temperature. Store in an airtight container at room temperature.

Prepare the Maple Vinaigrette: In a mixing bowl, combine all ingredients except the olive oil. Stir until well blended. Add the olive oil, and blend lightly. Refrigerate in an airtight container for up to 2 months. Mix well before each use.

To assemble the salad, combine the spinach, lettuce and beets in a salad bowl. Add the maple vinaigrette and toss to coat. Mound high on 4 plates, making sure the beets are not stuck together and are mixed in well with the lettuce and spinach. Top the lettuce with the pickled onions, dried cranberries, blue cheese and walnuts, in that order.

WINE:

The "life is too short" pick:
FX Pichler, Grüner Veltliner, Smaragd, Urgestein Terrassen, Wachau, Austria 2008
The "just because it's inexpensive doesn't mean you're cheap" pick:
Ecker, Grüner Veltliner, Wagram, Austria 2009
Alternatives: *A dry white wine with a ripe fruit edge and earthy notes. Australian Clare Valley Riesling or dry Washington Riesling.*

COLESLAW

SERVES 8

DRESSING

⅔ cup mayonnaise

1 tablespoon plus 1 teaspoon white wine vinegar

2 tablespoons plus 2 teaspoons half-and-half

2 teaspoons sugar

½ teaspoon kosher salt

⅛ teaspoon freshly ground black pepper

1 teaspoon dried whole dill

SALAD

3 cups shredded white cabbage (⅛-inch strips)

½ cup shredded carrots (⅛-inch strips)

2 tablespoons black raisins or dried currants

¼ cup golden raisins

Prepare the dressing: Place all the ingredients in a mixing bowl and stir until well blended.

Store, covered, in the refrigerator for 24 hours to let the flavors blend.

To assemble the salad, combine the cabbage, carrots and raisins in a bowl. Add the dressing and toss to blend.

Refrigerate for at least 2 hours to let the flavors blend. This can be made up to 24 hours in advance but may need to have some of the liquid drained off.

Note: If you prefer a crispy coleslaw, serve within 30 minutes of dressing.

I will always have a place in my heart for my mom's food, simple foods with great flavor. The coleslaw and potato recipes on this page are excellent examples of her cuisine, which I will continue to crave all of my life.

CLASSIC POTATO SALAD

SERVES 8

4 cups cooked russet potato pieces – bake the potatoes, then cool, peel, and cut into ½- to ⅝-inch pieces

½ cup diced celery (¼-inch pieces)

½ cup diced white or Walla Walla sweet onion (¼-inch pieces)

6 tablespoons sliced pitted black Cerignola olives

½ cup diced dill pickle (¼- to ⅜-inch pieces)

1 teaspoon celery seed

3 hard-boiled eggs, diced in ¼-inch pieces

1 teaspoon sea salt

½ teaspoon freshly ground black pepper

1¼ cups mayonnaise – Best Foods or, better yet, homemade

Combine all the ingredients and stir until well blended.

Chill overnight, allowing the flavors to blend.

GARLIC CROUTONS
MAKES 120 CROUTONS

5 slices white bread, deli-loaf style
2 tablespoons unsalted butter
2 tablespoons olive oil
1½ teaspoons granulated garlic
1 tablespoon very, very finely minced fresh garlic
½ teaspoon kosher salt

Set the bread out and let it stale, at least 2 to 3 hours, or until a crisp exterior has formed. You can hasten this process by placing the bread in an oven on the lowest temperature possible. But you must watch it carefully, as you don't want it to brown. Remove the crust and cut the bread into ¾-by-¾-inch cubes. Place the cubes in a bowl.

Preheat the oven to 375°F.

In a small saucepan or sauté pan, melt the butter together with the olive oil over medium heat. Stir in the granulated garlic, minced garlic and salt. Let the mixture sit on very low heat for 5 minutes, allowing the butter and oil to absorb the flavors of the garlic.

Drizzle a third of the butter mixture evenly over the bread pieces, stirring frequently to coat. Repeat 2 more times, being sure that every individual crouton has some of the mixture on it.

Spread the bread cubes on a sheet pan(s) in a single layer. Don't overcrowd the pan, or they will not brown properly. Bake for 5 minutes, then remove from the oven and toss on the pan. Return to the oven and cook for another 5 to 8 minutes, or until golden brown (the croutons will become bitter and hard if they are browned too much).

Remove and let cool to room temperature. Store tightly wrapped at room temperature until needed.

FRUIT COCKTAIL MOJITO STYLE
SERVES 4

1 cup diced fresh mango (½-inch cubes)
1½ cups diced fresh pineapple (½-inch cubes)
½ cup diced fresh papaya (½-inch cubes)
½ cup diced fresh kiwi (¼-inch cubes)
24 fresh whole raspberries
4 fresh mint sprigs

MOJITO DRESSING
3 tablespoons fresh lime juice
⅜ cup sugar
2 ounces Myers's dark rum
1 teaspoon thinly sliced fresh mint

Prepare the Mojito Dressing: Combine the lime juice and sugar, stirring until the sugar is completely dissolved. Stir in the rum and then add the mint. Use immediately.

Toss the tropical fruits together with the dressing. Then add the raspberries and lightly toss. Place in martini glasses and garnish with mint sprigs.

This can be refrigerated for up to 30 minutes before serving.

HOLLANDAISE SAUCE
MAKES 2 CUPS

4 fresh egg yolks
1½ teaspoons dry white wine
14 ounces unsalted butter, at room temperature
½ teaspoon Tabasco sauce
¼ teaspoon kosher salt

In a mixing bowl, whisk together the egg yolks and wine. Add the butter. Place the mixing bowl in a saucepan of simmering water, creating a double boiler. Whisking constantly, heat the mixture over hot water until thickened. Be sure to keep whisking the sauce so not to cook the egg. Remove from the heat as often as needed to prevent the sauce from sticking to the bottom. Occasionally lift the bowl off the saucepan to ensure that the egg mixture does not cook too rapidly on the bottom and sides of the bowl, scrambling the eggs.

Add the Tabasco sauce and salt. Stir well.

Keep warm and use within 2 to 4 hours.

Classic hollandaise sauce is made with clarified butter; this is a simpler version with great flavor. It works well with the classic hollandaise dishes such as eggs Benedict and in oysters Rockefeller, or over steamed asparagus or broccoli. It's also a nice base for creating flavored sauces like the Sweet Chili Hollandaise on page 151.

BASIL-GARLIC BUTTER

10 tablespoons salted butter, softened
1 tablespoon packed coarsely chopped fresh basil
1 teaspoon packed coarsely chopped fresh parsley
1½ teaspoons very, very finely minced fresh garlic
1½ teaspoons very, very finely minced fresh shallots
1 tablespoon fresh lemon juice

Whip the softened butter in a mixer with a wire whip until it peaks and turns light in color. Add all the remaining ingredients and whip until well blended.

Refrigerate until needed.

BUTTER SAUCE
MAKES ½ CUP

2 tablespoons whipping cream
½ cup unsalted butter, cut into 1-tablespoon pieces
¼ teaspoon kosher salt

Place the cream in a saucepan over low heat. When it is bubbling slowly, add the butter. When the butter has melted, stir in the salt. (If the sauce is too thick at this point, you can slowly stir in some warm water to thin it to the proper consistency.)

Keep the sauce warm until needed.

GARLIC AIOLI
MAKES 1½ CUPS

3 tablespoons egg yolks
1 whole large egg
⅜ teaspoon powdered fennel seed
1 tablespoon minced fresh garlic
1 tablespoon plus 1½ teaspoons minced
    Roasted Garlic (page 23)
1½ teaspoons Dijon mustard
3 tablespoons dry white wine – Altesse or
    Sauvignon Blanc
1 tablespoon fresh lemon juice
1 tablespoon very finely minced fresh parsley
1 teaspoon kosher salt
⅞ cup olive oil

Place the egg yolks and egg in a food processor or blender. Whip at high speed until they begin to thicken.

Add the fennel seed, fresh and roasted garlic, mustard, wine, lemon juice, parsley and salt. Combine well.

With the blender running at high speed, slowly drizzle in the olive oil, so the sauce will thicken and become well emulsified.

Refrigerate for at least 24 hours to allow the flavors to blend and the sauce to thicken.

BEURRE BLANC
MAKES 1 CUP

1 cup Chablis or similar dry white wine
2 tablespoons white wine vinegar
1 tablespoon finely minced fresh shallots
½ cup whipping cream
¾ pound unsalted butter, cut into 2-inch cubes
½ teaspoon kosher salt
Ground white pepper, to taste

Combine the wine, vinegar and shallots in a saucepan. Cook over medium-high heat until reduced to a light syrup consistency (approximately 90 percent).

Add the cream and cook over medium-high heat until reduced by 60 percent.

Reduce the heat to low and gradually add the butter cubes, stirring until melted.

Strain the sauce through a fine mesh strainer. Season with the salt and pepper. Keep warm until needed.

Note: When reducing sauces, I often use a percentage to indicate what the reduction should be. It is difficult to give a time frame, as the temperature being used to reduce the sauce may be quite different from one cook to another.

FRESH TOMATO SALSA
MAKES 2 CUPS

1 cup hand-diced ripe but firm Roma tomato (¼-inch pieces), with seeds and juice
½ cup hand-minced white onion (⅛-inch pieces)
2½ teaspoons fresh lime juice
1 teaspoon seeded and very finely minced jalapeño
½ teaspoon seeded and very finely minced habanero chile
1¾ teaspoons kosher salt
1 tablespoon olive oil
¼ cup tomato sauce
¼ cup tomato puree
1 tablespoon coarsely chopped fresh cilantro

In a bowl, combine all the ingredients and toss together until they are well coated.
Place in the refrigerator and chill for 2 hours, which allows the flavors to blend.

This is my family's favorite snack food. I have to make it a gallon at a time. It is a great salsa with chips, grilled chicken or fish. In the summertime when heirloom tomatoes are prevalent, substitute those for Romas. The bright colors make it even more fun.

TERIYAKI MARINADE
MAKES 1 QUART

3 cups hot water
1½ cups packed light brown sugar
3 cups soy sauce
4 tablespoons finely minced peeled fresh ginger
2 teaspoons finely minced fresh garlic
2 tablespoons dry vermouth
½ cup pineapple juice
2 tablespoons sliced green onions
     (⅛-inch pieces)

The water must be hot enough to dissolve the sugar; heat it if necessary. Combine the water, sugar and soy sauce. Stir until the sugar is completely dissolved.

Add the ginger, garlic, vermouth and pineapple juice. Stir to blend. Let cool, then add the green onions.

Store in a covered container in the refrigerator for up to 4 months.

VEAL DEMI-GLACE
MAKES 1 CUP

1 tablespoon canola oil
¼ cup chopped yellow onion (¼-inch pieces)
2 tablespoons chopped carrot (¼-inch pieces)
8 ounces celery, chopped in ¼-inch pieces
½ teaspoon sugar
1 tablespoon plus 1½ teaspoons tomato paste
½ cup red wine (Cabernet or Merlot)
5 cups Veal Brown Stock (page 121)

Place the oil in a large saucepan over medium-high heat. Add the onion, carrot and celery. Sear until lightly browned. Add the sugar and cook until completely caramelized — but do not char or burn, as it will make the sauce bitter.

Add the tomato paste and wine. Bring to a simmer and cook until reduced by 75 percent, approximately 3 to 4 minutes.

Add the veal stock and bring to a gentle simmer. Let simmer and reduce for 2 hours, skimming every 15 to 20 minutes. Strain and discard the vegetables.

Return the stock to the heat, bring to a low simmer, and reduce over medium-low heat until it has a medium-thick consistency and the volume has reduced to 1 cup.

Strain through a chinois (fine-mesh strainer). Refrigerate until needed.

Note: To store the demi-glace longer, freeze in an ice-cube tray, then transfer the cubes to a resealable plastic freezer bag. It will keep for up to 6 months.

Red Chili Rice
Makes 3 cups (4 servings)

1 tablespoon plus 1 teaspoon canola oil
¼ cup minced white onion
1½ teaspoons minced fresh garlic
1 cup long-grain white rice
4 tablespoons tomato paste
1¾ cups Vegetable Stock (page 118)
½ teaspoon kosher salt
¼ teaspoon ground cumin
¼ teaspoon paprika
¾ teaspoon ancho chili powder
¼ teaspoon dried whole oregano leaves
2 tablespoons peeled, seeded and diced roasted red jalapeños (⅛-inch pieces)
½ teaspoon pureed chipotle peppers in adobo sauce
½ cup coarsely chopped roasted corn kernels (page 98)
2 tablespoons coarsely chopped fresh cilantro

Preheat the oven to 400°F.

Place the oil, onion and garlic in a sauté pan over medium heat. Cook until just tender, then add the rice and toss until completely coated. Add the tomato paste and toss until coated and beginning to brown. Transfer the mixture to an 8-by-8- or 10-by-8-inch glass baking dish.

In a saucepan, combine the vegetable stock, salt, cumin, paprika, chili powder, oregano, jalapeños and chipotle. Heat until lightly steaming but not simmering (170°F). Pour the stock into the rice and stir well.

Cover tightly with foil and bake for 25 minutes. Uncover and fluff with a fork. Stir in the roasted corn and cilantro.

CILANTRO RICE

MAKES 3 CUPS (4 SERVINGS)

1⅓ cups long-grain white rice
1 tablespoon canola oil
2 cups Vegetable Stock (page 118)
1½ teaspoons kosher salt
1 tablespoon fresh lime juice
1 tablespoon salted butter
1 tablespoon chopped fresh cilantro (¼- to ⅜-inch pieces)

CILANTRO PUREE

2 tablespoons canola oil
2 teaspoons very finely minced fresh garlic
2 teaspoons seeded, coarsely chopped fresh jalapeño
¼ cup packed chopped fresh cilantro
1 teaspoon ground coriander

Prepare the Cilantro Puree: In a blender or mini food processor, combine all the ingredients. Blend until completely pureed.

If the puree is not being used immediately, transfer to a container with a tight-fitting lid. Place plastic wrap over the puree, pressing it directly against the puree. Close the container and store in the refrigerator.

To prepare the rice, preheat the oven to 400°F.

In a bowl, combine the rice, canola oil and cilantro puree. Mix until the rice is completely coated. Transfer to an 8-by-8-inch glass baking dish.

Bring the vegetable stock and salt to a boil. Pour into the rice and stir well. Add the lime juice.

Cover tightly with foil and bake for 30 minutes. Uncover and fluff with a fork. Use immediately, or let cool, refrigerate until needed, and reheat by steaming.

To serve, add the butter and chopped cilantro, and stir lightly.

CITRUS RICE
MAKES 3 CUPS (4 SERVINGS)

2½ cups Vegetable Stock (page 118)
2 tablespoons wheat berries
1½ cups jasmine rice
1 tablespoon canola oil
1 tablespoon minced shallot
1 tablespoon plus 1 teaspoon freshly minced lemon zest
2 tablespoons fresh lemon juice
½ teaspoon kosher salt
¾ teaspoon sea salt
¼ teaspoon freshly ground black pepper
3 tablespoons salted butter, cut into pieces
1 tablespoon finely minced Preserved Lemon (page 47)
1½ teaspoons coarsely chopped fresh chervil
1 tablespoon coarsely chopped fresh Italian parsley

In a saucepan, bring the vegetable stock to a boil, then add the wheat berries. Turn off the heat and let steep for 15 minutes.

Preheat the oven to 400°F.

Mix the rice, oil and shallots together thoroughly in a small (4- to 6-cup) baking pan, coating the rice grains well with oil. Bring the stock and wheat berries back to a boil and pour into the rice. Add the lemon zest, lemon juice and kosher salt, stirring well.

Cover tightly with foil and bake for 25 to 30 minutes. Uncover and fluff with a fork. Stir in the sea salt, pepper, butter, preserved lemon and herbs.

POTATO GNOCCHI
MAKES 3½ POUNDS

2 tablespoons kosher salt
1 pound russet potatoes, washed clean
3 large egg yolks
½ cup grated Parmigiano-Reggiano cheese
¼ teaspoon freshly grated nutmeg
½ teaspoon pink sea salt
¼ teaspoon freshly ground black pepper
1 cup all-purpose flour, plus more for dusting

Special equipment: parchment paper or waxed paper; gnocchi board (optional); electric fan

Preheat the oven to 425°F.

Spread the salt evenly across a baking sheet (this prevents the potatoes from overcooking on the bottom). Place the potatoes on the sheet and bake until slightly overcooked, approximately 45 to 55 minutes, to an internal temperature of 165-175°F.

Line several baking sheets with parchment paper or waxed paper.

Let the potatoes sit until cool enough to handle, then cut in half and remove the flesh.

Pass the potato meat through a potato ricer, or grate through the large holes of a box grater. This should yield about 2 cups of potato.

Mound the potatoes on a lightly floured countertop. Make a well in the center and add the egg yolks, cheese, nutmeg, salt and pepper. Mix into the potatoes and blend well with your hands.

Sprinkle half of the flour over the potatoes and, using your knuckles, press it into the potatoes. Fold the mass over on itself and press down again. Add the remaining flour a little at a time, folding and pressing the dough until it just holds together — do not knead the dough, as this will make the gnocchi tough.

Work any dough clinging to your fingers back into the dough. If the mixture is too dry (slightly crumbling), add a little water. The dough should give under slight pressure. It will feel firm but still be yielding. To test for the correct consistency, take a piece of dough and roll it with your hands on a well-floured surface into a ½-inch-diameter rope. If the dough holds its shape, it is ready. If not, add more flour, fold and press the dough several more times, and test again. Try not to overwork the dough.

Keeping your work surface and the dough lightly floured, cut the dough into 4 equal pieces. Roll each piece into a ½-inch-diameter rope. Cut into ½-inch-long pieces. Lightly flour the gnocchi as you cut them.

You can cook these as they are or form them into the classic gnocchi shape with a gnocchi board, or the tines of a large fork turned upside down. Rest the bottom edge of the gnocchi board on the work surface, then tilt it at about a 45-degree angle. Take each piece of dough and squish it lightly with your thumb against the board while simultaneously pushing it away from you. It will roll away and around your thumb, taking on a cupped shape — with ridges on the outer curve from the board and a smooth surface on the inner curve where your thumb was. Shaping the gnocchi is a skill and may take some time to master. The indentation allows the gnocchi to hold sauces better and cook faster. As you shape the gnocchi, dust them lightly with flour and scatter them on the prepared baking sheets.

Set the gnocchi-filled baking sheets in front of a fan on low speed for 30 minutes, turning the gnocchi after 15 minutes. Refrigerate the gnocchi until needed.

If you are not going to cook the gnocchi that day, freeze them. They can be cooked from a frozen state, but they cook better and faster when thawed.

When ready to use, place the gnocchi in boiling water and cook until tender, approximately 2 to 3 minutes. When cooked completely, the gnocchi will float.

CIPOLLINI ONIONS AU GRATIN
SERVES 8 TO 10

2 pounds cipollini onions, peeled
1 quart Chicken Stock (page 120)
½ teaspoon sea salt
1 bay leaf
1 teaspoon dried whole thyme leaves
1 teaspoon pureed roasted garlic (page 23)
1 cup Chablis or other dry white wine
3 cups heavy cream

AU GRATIN CHEESE MIX
¼ cup coarsely shredded Jack cheese
¼ cup coarsely shredded Cheddar cheese
¼ cup coarsely shredded Gouda cheese
¼ cup grated Parmesan cheese
¼ cup fine dry bread crumbs

Prepare the Au Gratin Cheese Mix: Combine all the ingredients and mix until well blended. Refrigerate until needed.

To prepare the onions, place the onions, chicken stock, salt, bay leaf, thyme and roasted garlic in a large saucepan. Bring to a simmer over medium heat and cook for 5 to 8 minutes, or until tender. Remove from the heat and set aside.

With a slotted spoon, transfer the onions to a 10-by-8-inch baking dish, arranging them so they cover the bottom.

Place the cooking broth back on the stove and bring to a simmer over medium-high heat. Add the wine, lower the heat to medium, and simmer until reduced by 75 percent.

Add the cream and cook until reduced by 50 percent. Remove from the heat and let the sauce cool.

Preheat the oven to 325°F.

Cover the onions with the sauce, top with the au gratin cheese mix, and bake for 15 minutes, or until the top is golden brown and the edges are bubbling. Remove from the oven and let cool slightly.

TRUFFLE MASHED POTATOES
SERVES 4

1½ pounds Yukon Gold potatoes, peeled and quartered
2 ounces unsalted butter
½ cup half-and-half
¾ teaspoon sea or kosher salt
¼ teaspoon ground white pepper
¼ ounce black truffles, fresh or frozen, sliced thin and then cut into 1/16-inch strips
1 tablespoon white truffle oil

Boil the potatoes until fully cooked, approximately 15 to 20 minutes. Drain completely and let sit until they are dry on the exterior. Place the potatoes in a mixer. Using a paddle attachment, start to mix on medium speed to break up the potatoes.

Melt the butter and half-and-half together, then slowly add to the potatoes.

Switch to the whip attachment and whip the potatoes until creamy. Whip in the seasonings, truffles and truffle oil.

Keep hot until needed.

Note: If you prefer a slightly creamier potato, use a ricer on the potatoes before whipping.

CREAMY RUSSET POTATO HASH
SERVES 8

4 cups peeled russet potatoes cut in ½-inch dice (about 2 very large russets)
¼ cup plus 2 tablespoons grated Parmesan/Fontina (50/50) cheese blend, divided
½ teaspoon sea salt
¼ teaspoon freshly ground pepper
1 teaspoon minced fresh parsley

LEEK-ONION MIX
1 tablespoon olive oil
1 cup diced yellow onions (¼-inch pieces)
½ tablespoon minced fresh garlic
¼ cup sliced leeks – light green part only, sliced lengthwise and then crosswise
        into ¼-inch slices
½ teaspoon dried thyme leaves
¼ cup Chablis or similar white wine

SOUR CREAM SAUCE
1½ cups Vegetable Stock (page 118)
¾ cup whipping cream
1½ bay leaves
3 tablespoons salted butter
3 tablespoons flour
¾ cup sour cream
1½ teaspoons sea or kosher salt
¹⁄₁₆ teaspoon ground white pepper

Prepare the Leek-Onion Mix: Heat the olive oil in a saucepan over medium-high heat. Add the onions, garlic and leeks. Sauté until tender. Add the thyme, reduce the heat to low, and cook for 3 minutes.

Add the wine and let reduce for 3 minutes. Let cool, then refrigerate until needed. This will keep, covered, for several days.

Prepare the Sour Cream Sauce: In a saucepan, combine the vegetable stock, whipping cream and bay leaves, stirring well to blend. Heat over medium-high heat until the mixture starts to simmer, then lower the heat to medium.

In a heavy-gauge saucepan, melt the butter over medium heat. Add the flour, stirring to create a roux. Let the roux cook for 3 to 4 minutes. Do not scorch.

Slowly whisk the warm stock mixture into the roux. After all the stock has been added, continue to cook for 10 minutes, or until the sauce becomes thick and creamy.

Turn off the heat and blend in the sour cream, salt and pepper. Let cool, then refrigerate until needed.

To prepare the hash: Preheat the oven to 400°F.

Spray the bottom of a 12-by-9-inch pan with cooking spray.

In a large bowl, combine the potatoes, 2 tablespoons of the grated cheese blend, salt, pepper, the Leek-Onion Mix and three-quarters of the Sour Cream Sauce. Toss to blend. Place in the pan and top with the remaining sauce.

Cover the pan with foil; cut a 1-inch slit in the center. Bake for 50 to 60 minutes, or until the potatoes are just fork tender.

Remove from the oven, cut a few more slits in the foil, and let cool to room temperature. Refrigerate until needed.

Note: This can be made and stored, covered, in the refrigerator for 3 to 4 days.

To serve, preheat the oven to 375°F. Top the potatoes with the remaining ¼ cup of the grated cheese blend. Reheat in the oven for 15 to 20 minutes, or until the internal temperature is 140°F and the cheese topping is golden brown.

Sprinkle with minced parsley and cut into serving portions.

SOUTHWESTERN ROASTED CORN MASHED POTATOES
SERVES 4

1 tablespoon salted butter
½ cup Roasted Corn
1 pound Yukon Gold Mashed Potatoes
1½ teaspoons Southwestern Seasoning Mix

SOUTHWESTERN SEASONING MIX
MAKES ½ CUP
2 tablespoons kosher salt
1 tablespoon plus 1½ teaspoons ancho chili powder
½ teaspoon cayenne pepper
2 tablespoons plus ½ teaspoon mild chili powder
2 tablespoons plus ½ teaspoon sweet paprika
1 teaspoon ground white pepper

ROASTED CORN
MAKES 1 CUP
1 fresh ear of corn
1½ teaspoons olive oil
¼ teaspoon kosher salt

Prepare the Southwestern Seasoning Mix: Combine all the ingredients and mix until well blended. Store in an airtight container at room temperature for up to 3 months.

Prepare the Roasted Corn: Remove the husk and silk from the corn. Brush the corn with the olive oil, then season with salt.

Roast over medium-high heat on an outdoor grill or in a grill pan, or over an open flame, for about 2½ to 3 minutes, making a quarter turn every 30 seconds or so, until the corn is golden brown and slightly charred. Some of the kernels should be caramelized through the skin, and some exposed kernels will be slightly charred.

Let cool, then cut the kernels off the cob. Refrigerate until needed.

To prepare the potatoes, melt the butter in a sauté pan over medium-high heat. Add the roasted corn kernels and sauté until tender. Add the mashed potatoes and the seasoning mix, and fold together until heated through.

YUKON GOLD MASHED POTATOES

YIELD: 1 POUND (2-3 SERVINGS)
1 pound Yukon Gold potatoes, peeled and quartered
6 tablespoons unsalted butter
6 tablespoons half-and-half
½ teaspoon kosher salt
⅛ teaspoon ground white pepper

YIELD: 1½ POUNDS (4 SERVINGS)
1½ pounds Yukon Gold potatoes, peeled and quartered
½ cup unsalted butter
½ cup half-and-half
¾ teaspoon kosher salt
¼ teaspoon ground white pepper

YIELD: 2 POUNDS (5-6 SERVINGS)
2 pounds Yukon Gold potatoes, peeled and quartered
¾ cup unsalted butter
¾ cup half-and-half
1 teaspoon kosher salt
¼ teaspoon ground white pepper

Boil the potatoes until fully cooked and tender, approximately 15 to 20 minutes. Drain well.

In a heavy-gauge saucepan, combine the butter and half-and-half. Warm over medium heat until the butter is melted, being careful not to brown. Reserve and keep warm until needed.

Place the potatoes in a countertop mixer. Using the paddle attachment, mix to break up the potatoes. Then switch to the whip attachment and whip on medium-high speed, gradually adding the butter-cream liquid.

Add the salt and pepper, and whip the potatoes on medium speed until mashed and creamy. Serve immediately, or keep warm until needed, up to 2 hours.

Note: There will be some lumps in the potatoes. If you like a creamier consistency, run the potatoes through a ricer before placing in the mixer.

POTATO LASAGNA WITH CARAMELIZED ONIONS
SERVES 12

4 tablespoons clarified butter, divided (page 135)
3 cups very thinly sliced Walla Walla Sweet onions
4 pounds russet potatoes, peeled and sliced ⅛ inch thick
2 teaspoons sea or kosher salt
1 teaspoon freshly ground pepper
½ cup grated Parmigiano-Reggiano cheese

SOUR CREAM SAUCE
1 cup Vegetable Stock (page 118)
½ cup whipping cream
1 bay leaf
2 tablespoons salted butter
2 tablespoons flour
½ cup sour cream
1 teaspoon sea or kosher salt
1/16 teaspoon ground white pepper

Prepare the Sour Cream Sauce: In a saucepan, combine the vegetable stock, whipping cream and bay leaf, stirring to blend well. Heat over medium-high heat until the mixture starts to simmer, then lower the heat to medium.

In a heavy-gauge saucepan, melt the butter over medium heat. Add the flour, stirring to create a roux. Let the roux cook for 3 to 4 minutes. Do not scorch.

Slowly whisk the warm stock mixture into the roux. When all the stock has been added, continue to cook for 10 minutes, or until the sauce becomes thick and creamy.

Turn off the heat and blend in the sour cream, salt and pepper. Let cool, then refrigerate until needed.

Prepare the Potato Lasagna: Place 2 tablespoons of the clarified butter in a sauté pan over medium heat. Add the onions and cook, stirring constantly, until they are tender and lightly caramelized. Remove from the heat and let cool.

Preheat the oven to 325°F.

Using a 4-inch-deep 12-by-9-inch baking dish, baste the bottom and sides of the pan completely with 1 tablespoon clarified butter. Layer a quarter of the potatoes on the bottom of the pan. Season with a third of the salt and pepper. Next, layer a third of the caramelized onions. Then add a third of the sour cream sauce and 2 tablespoons of the grated cheese. Follow this procedure two more times. Then top with the remaining potatoes and baste with 1 tablespoon clarified butter.

Cover with foil and bake for 60 minutes. Remove the foil and top with the remaining grated cheese. Increase the oven temperature to 375°F, then return the pan to the oven and bake, uncovered, for 15 minutes, or until the cheese is light golden brown. Remove from the oven, let cool slightly, then cut into 3-inch squares and serve.

WINE:
The "life is too short" pick:
Domaine du Vieux Télégraphe,
Châteauneuf-du-Pape,
Rhône, France 2007
The "just because it's inexpensive doesn't mean you're cheap" pick:
Syncline, Grenache-Carignan,
Columbia Valley, Washington 2009
Alternatives: *An earthy red with moderate-plus tannin, herbal notes and rich fruit. Australian Grenache/ Syrah or California Syrah.*

It was neat to watch how Debbie tempers him as a person and see him become much more fulfilled personally, to see him raise the boys and have a family. He can maintain his hard-driven style, but he is such a softhearted person on the other side of it. I had been at home raising kids for a while and wanted to go back to work. John was opening Seastar, we were living in Edmonds, and I agreed to commute because I was excited to work for John. One of the neatest things about working for him is not only the excitement of what he provides as a chef, but also that his work environment is so family friendly. He truly takes care of his managers. I was allowed to pretty much work around my family needs. He does a good job with work/life balance. The restaurant business usually doesn't allow that, but John made time for coaching the boys, his church, taking his family on vacation. He sets that example, and he truly provides that for his managers. He's like a walking computer. He accomplishes so much, it's amazing.

KATHI JO MENZYK
LONGTIME FRIEND

Before the restaurant opened, John was having a staff meeting. He told them we were not going to be open on Thanksgiving, Christmas Eve or Christmas Day. He said there were people crying — they just don't get that in the restaurant business. So before we even opened, they knew he valued their family life, their personal life, as well as his own.

DEBBIE HOWIE
WIFE, SOULMATE

Soups & Stocks

CRAB AND CORN BISQUE
SERVES 4

½ pound unsalted butter
½ cup very finely minced white onion
2 tablespoons very finely minced shallot
1 cup clam juice
¾ cup corn kernels, fresh or frozen (see note)
¼ cup flour
½ cup dry sherry
2 quarts half-and-half
½ teaspoon ground dried thyme
2 teaspoons sea salt
½ teaspoon ground white pepper

PORT-MADEIRA REDUCTION
MAKES ¼ CUP
½ cup Madeira
½ cup tawny Port
2 tablespoons balsamic vinegar
2 tablespoons sugar

For serving:
12 ounces fresh Dungeness crab meat
2 tablespoons Port-Madeira Reduction
1 tablespoon diagonally sliced chives
     (¾-inch pieces)

Melt the butter over medium heat in a large pot. Add the onions and shallots, and sauté until semitranslucent.

In a blender, combine the clam juice and corn. Blend until completely pureed. Set aside.

Add the flour to the pot, stirring to create a roux. Cook for 2 to 3 minutes, stirring constantly so it doesn't brown.

Add the sherry and cook, stirring, for 30 seconds to deglaze the pan. Gradually add the half-and-half, stirring constantly. Bring to a simmer, continuing to stir constantly.

Add the pureed corn/clam juice mixture to the pot and bring to a simmer.

Lower the heat and add the thyme, salt and pepper. Simmer, stirring constantly, until it has thickened. The consistency should be slightly thicker than that of heavy cream. Remove from the heat and cool in an ice bath. Refrigerate until needed (see note).

Prepare the Port-Madeira Reduction: Combine all the ingredients in a saucepan and bring to a boil. Cook until reduced to a quarter of the original volume. Let cool, then refrigerate until needed (see note).

To serve, place 48 ounces (6 cups) of the bisque in a pot. Bring to a boil quickly, add the crab, and pour into bowls. Drizzle the reduction back and forth across the bowls. Garnish with the chives.

Note: Fresh corn is preferable, but frozen can be substituted. Do not use canned corn, as the bisque is thickened by the starch from the corn. Canned corn has the starch cooked out of it.

Note: There will be some leftover bisque — it will keep for up to 4 days in the refrigerator.

Note: Leftover Port-Madeira Reduction can be served with roasted chicken or grilled pork chops. It is also delicious drizzled on cheeses such as Brie or Délice de Bourgogne.

WINE:
Barbeito, Malvasia, Madeira 1954
Alternatives: *A dry, nutty, slightly sweet fortified wine. Pedro Ximénez from Spain.*

Matching wine with soup can be a challenging exercise because they are both liquid, but it's much easier if you follow the rule of "body balancing." Add a little "texture" with the wine.

PORCINI MUSHROOM SOUP WITH TRUFFLE CRÈME
SERVES 8

1 ounce dried porcini mushrooms
1 quart Vegetable Stock (page 118)
½ cup unsalted butter
¼ cup flour
¾ cup grated white or cremini mushroom caps and/or stems (¹⁄₁₆-inch)
¼ cup sliced cremini mushrooms (⅛ inch thick)
2 tablespoons sliced shiitake mushrooms (⅛ inch thick)
1½ teaspoons kosher salt
¼ teaspoon ground black pepper
2¼ teaspoons chopped fresh tarragon
2 cups whipping cream
2 teaspoons sliced chives (⅛-inch pieces), for garnish

TRUFFLE CRÈME
¼ cup whipping cream
⅛ teaspoon sea salt
1½ teaspoons truffle-infused olive oil

Soak the dried porcini in the vegetable stock for 1 hour. Then strain off the liquid and reserve. Finely mince the porcini.

Melt the butter in a stockpot over medium-low heat. Add the flour to create a roux, reduce the heat to very low, and cook for 5 to 7 minutes, stirring constantly so it doesn't brown.

In a separate pan, heat the reserved mushroom-vegetable stock to just below a simmer. Then slowly stir the stock into the roux. When all the stock has been added, increase the heat slightly and bring to a simmer. When the soup begins to thicken, reduce the heat and let simmer for 20 to 30 minutes.

Add all the fresh and reconstituted mushrooms. Then add the salt and pepper. Cook for another 10 minutes on a low simmer, then add the tarragon and cream. Serve, or let cool and then refrigerate until needed.

Prepare the Truffle Crème: Combine all the ingredients in a mixing bowl and whip with a whisk until creamy and medium stiff.

To serve, top each bowl of soup with truffle crème and chives.

WINE:
Lustau Rare Cream Sherry Solera Reserva, Jerez, Andalucia, Spain
Alternatives: Pair the soup with a fortified wine with off-dry richness. Ten-year-old Tawny Port.

HOT AND SOUR THAI SHRIMP SOUP

SERVES 4 AS AN ENTRÉE

6 ⅔ cups Chicken Stock (page 120)
⅓ cup lemongrass sliced in 1-inch pieces (white part only, smashed)
1 tablespoon chopped galangal (skin on)
5 fresh kaffir lime leaves, sliced in ¼-inch strips
2 tablespoons plus 1 teaspoon Thai fish sauce
1½ teaspoons sambal oelek (chili paste)
1 cup Mae Ploy Thai chili paste in oil with shrimp (see note)
1½ teaspoons salt
2¼ cups canned diced tomatoes in juice, drained
3 cups canned straw mushrooms, drained
3 tablespoons plus 1½ teaspoons fresh lime juice

For serving:
1 cup peeled and chopped white Gulf shrimp (½- to ¾-inch pieces)
8 fresh kaffir lime leaves
2 tablespoons plus 2 teaspoons fresh lime juice
2 tablespoons plus 2 teaspoons very coarsely chopped fresh cilantro

Place the stock, lemongrass, galangal and kaffir lime leaves in a stockpot. Bring to a boil, then reduce the heat to very low, cover, and simmer for 4 hours. Strain the stock and remove the lemongrass, galangal and lime leaves.

To the strained stock add the fish sauce, sambal oelek, chili paste in oil and salt. Cook over medium heat for 5 minutes. Add the tomatoes and mushrooms, and cook for 5 minutes. Add the lime juice. Let cool, then refrigerate or use immediately (see note).

To serve, place 48 ounces (6 cups) of the soup base in a large saucepan, add the shrimp, and bring to a boil. Remove from the heat.

Place 2 kaffir lime leaves in each bowl, then pour the soup into the bowls, being sure to distribute the shrimp, mushrooms and tomatoes evenly. Add the lime juice to the soup and top with cilantro.

Notes:
This is a classic Thai recipe from the family of my Seastar Raw Bar chef David Putaportiwon. We have made some minor adjustments, but it is important to use the specified ingredients to achieve the proper flavors.

Thai chili paste in oil with shrimp is essential to the integrity of the recipe. The brand could be different, but it is important to include this ingredient.

There will be some leftover soup base — it will keep for up to a week in the refrigerator.

WINE:
Renardat-Fache, Cerdon du Bugey, France
Alternatives: *A lightly sparkling, semi-sweet wine to balance the hot spice element of the soup.*
Moscato d'Asti from Italy.

OYSTER STEW
SERVES 4

¼ cup olive oil

4 tablespoons salted butter

½ cup diced leeks – white and light green parts only, sliced in
       half and then cut into ¼-inch pieces

1 cup diced white onions (¼-inch pieces)

1 cup diced peeled celery root (⅛-inch pieces)

½ cup Muscadet wine

3 cups whipping cream

½ teaspoon sea salt

¾ teaspoon freshly ground black pepper

36 oysters – Kusshi or Shigoku (see note)

1 cup half-and-half

4 fresh chervil sprigs

SAVORY GARLIC OYSTER CRACKERS

3 tablespoons salted butter

½ teaspoon minced fresh garlic

½ teaspoon granulated onion

1 teaspoon finely minced fresh Italian parsley

1 cup extra-large oyster crackers

⅛ teaspoon powdered sea salt
       (grind in a mini food processor or with a mortar and pestle)

CHERVIL-SAVORY MIX

2½ teaspoons chopped fresh chervil

¾ teaspoon chopped fresh savory

1 tablespoon chopped fresh Italian parsley

Special equipment: Silpat or parchment paper

Place the olive oil and butter in a large sauté pan over medium heat. Add the leeks, onions and celery root, and sauté lightly until translucent.

Add the wine. Then add the whipping cream, salt and pepper. Let simmer for 30 minutes, reducing slightly.

Using a handheld blender, puree the mixture. Refrigerate until needed.

Prepare the Savory Garlic Oyster Crackers: Preheat the oven to 350°F. Line a sheet pan with Silpat or parchment paper.

Melt the butter and garlic together in a saucepan over medium heat. Let cool slightly. Place in a mini food processor. Add the granulated onion and parsley. Process until completely pureed.

Transfer the mixture to a bowl, add the crackers and salt, and toss to blend. Spread the crackers on the prepared pan and bake for 8 to 10 minutes, or until golden brown. Remove from the oven and place on paper towels. Let cool, then store in an airtight container at room temperature until needed.

Prepare the Chervil-Savory Mix: Combine all the ingredients and stir to blend. Refrigerate until needed.

To serve the soup, shuck the oysters, reserving the oyster liquor (juices from the oysters).

Place the stew base and half-and-half in a soup pot over medium heat. When it is simmering, add the oysters with the oyster liquor. Let simmer for 1½ minutes.

Add the chervil-savory mix, and simmer for 30 seconds. Taste and adjust the seasoning as needed. The oysters' salt level will vary greatly, and you may want to add a little salt or pepper.

Place the stew in 4 large bowls. Top with the oyster crackers and chervil sprigs.

Note: Shigoku and Kusshi oysters are very small and expensive. You can substitute another local oyster — a Pacific yearling such as a Penn Cove Select, for example. When substituting a slightly larger oyster, you will have to increase the cooking time by approximately 30 to 60 seconds.

WINE:
The "life is too short" pick:
Merry Edwards, Sauvignon Blanc, Russian River Valley, California 2010
The "just because it's inexpensive doesn't mean you're cheap" pick:
Efeste, Sauvignon Blanc, "Feral," Evergreen Vineyard, Columbia Valley, Washington 2010
Alternatives: *A super-crisp and fresh white with vibrant acidity and fresh citrus notes. New Zealand Sauvignon Blanc or French Sauvignon Blanc (Sancerre/Pouilly Fumé).*

TORTILLA SOUP WITH AVOCADO–ROASTED CORN RELISH
SERVES 4 AS AN ENTRÉE

SHREDDED CHICKEN

1 pound boneless, skinless chicken breasts,
    fat removed
2 cups Chicken Stock (page 120)

TORTILLA SOUP

3 tablespoons canola oil
1 tablespoon finely minced fresh garlic
2 tablespoons chopped fresh cilantro
5 six-inch corn tortillas, coarsely chopped
¾ cup finely minced onion
2 cups pureed fresh Roma tomatoes
½ cup peeled and minced roasted poblano
    peppers (see note, page 112)
2 quarts Chicken Stock (page 120)
1 tablespoon ground cumin
⅛ teaspoon cayenne pepper
1½ teaspoons ancho chili powder
½ teaspoon ground coriander
2 bay leaves
1 tablespoon double-concentrate tomato paste
1 teaspoon kosher or sea salt
1 tablespoon fresh lime juice
Crispy Tortilla Strips (page 112), for serving
4 fresh cilantro sprigs, for garnish

AVOCADO-ROASTED CORN RELISH

3 tablespoons diced white onion
    (⅛-inch pieces)
¼ cup seeded and diced Roma tomato
    (¼-inch pieces)
2 tablespoons diced ripe tomatillo
    (¼-inch pieces)
½ teaspoon seeded and minced fresh jalapeño
½ teaspoon fresh lime juice
1½ teaspoons coarsely chopped fresh cilantro
¼ teaspoon kosher salt
½ teaspoon olive oil
¼ cup diced firm ripe avocado (½-inch pieces)
¼ cup roasted corn kernels (page 98)

Prepare the Shredded Chicken: Place the breasts in the stock and cook on a slow simmer until the chicken is cooked through. Remove the chicken from the stock and let cool. Pull off pieces of meat in ⅛-inch-thick by 1- to 2-inch-long strings. Refrigerate until needed.

Prepare the Tortilla Soup: Heat the oil over medium-high heat in a large soup pot. Add the garlic, cilantro and tortilla pieces. Sauté until the tortillas are tender. Add the onion and pureed tomatoes. Bring to a boil, stirring constantly.

Add the poblanos, stock, spices, bay leaves, tomato paste, salt and lime juice. Bring to a boil, then reduce the heat and simmer for 30 minutes, stirring frequently and skimming the top if necessary. Remove the bay leaves with a slotted spoon.

Add the chicken to the soup. Let the soup cool, then refrigerate until needed.

Prepare the Avocado-Roasted Corn Relish: Combine all ingredients except the avocado and corn. Mix until the ingredients are well coated.

Just before using, stir in the avocado and corn.

To serve, reheat the soup to 165°F. Stir well and ladle into serving bowls. Top with the tortilla strips, then the relish and cilantro sprigs.

> **WINE:**
> ***Duval-Leroy, Brut, Vertus, France***
> Alternatives: *A dry sparkling wine with lifted
> acidity and a rich fruit core.
> California sparkling wine or
> Italian Prosecco.*

CRISPY TORTILLA STRIPS
MAKES 1 CUP

4 six-inch corn tortillas
Oil
¼ teaspoon kosher salt

Special equipment: deep fryer

Cut the tortillas in half and then into ⅛-inch strips.

Heat the oil in the deep fryer according to the manufacturer's instructions.

Place the tortilla strips in the deep fryer and cook until golden brown. Remove from the oil and let drain in a perforated pan lined with paper towels. Season the strips with the salt.

Keep in a covered container at room temperature until needed.

Note: There are several ways to roast poblano peppers. Using the oven broiler, cook until the skin is blackened, then turn them over and cook until blackened on the other side. Remove from the oven, let cool slightly, and place in a sealed plastic bag. After 15 minutes, remove from the bag, peel off the skin, and seed the peppers. You can also blacken a pepper over an open flame on a gas range or in a very hot oven. Follow the same procedure after the skin is blackened.

On Thanksgiving we serve families in need a full Thanksgiving dinner with all the trimmings. A couple of years ago, we had a guest who called and said, "We have a reservation for my family; we are a party of twelve. We are not going to be able to come because my mother is ill and she won't be able to make the trip. I might be able to get some of my family there, but I will need to change my numbers. I am calling you directly because I want to thank you for what you are doing, but I just don't know if I'm going to be able to make it, because I am going to be driving out to take care of my mother instead." John asked if we got her number, and then said to call her back and tell her that we will box the food up and if she can get someone to pick it up, she can take some out to her mother and leave some for her family. These were people who were really in a bad way. The woman was so overwhelmed, on the verge of homelessness, hungry, so many mouths to feed, losing her mother, medical bills — it's more than anybody should have to bear. And so, she did come. He had everything all boxed up and ready. Right on time, her car was parked outside. John carried it out to her. She said thank you. He wished her a Happy Thanksgiving and told her, "God bless you." As he turned around and started to walk away, he noticed she was still in the car and hadn't moved. He looked out the window and saw she still hadn't moved, and there she was, so overwhelmed. So he went out and sat in her car and held her hand until she was ready.

CATHY LALLEY
MARKETING DIRECTOR

FARMERS MARKET VEGETABLE BARLEY SOUP WITH HERBS
SERVES 6

¼ pound barley
2 quarts Vegetable Stock (page 118)
1 tablespoon olive oil
1½ teaspoons minced fresh garlic
½ cup diced sweet onion (¼-inch pieces)
½ cup sliced celery (¼-inch pieces)
2 cups V8 vegetable juice
1 bay leaf
1 tablespoon kosher salt
1 teaspoon coarsely ground black pepper
¾ teaspoon green Tabasco sauce
¾ cup sliced carrots (quartered lengthwise, then cut in ¼-inch slices)
½ cup sliced green beans (1-inch pieces)
½ cup fresh corn kernels
¾ cup diced heirloom tomatoes (½-inch pieces), assorted colors
½ cup sliced green or yellow zucchini (halved lengthwise, then cut in ½-inch slices)
½ cup peas or sliced snow peas or sugar snap peas
2 tablespoons chopped fresh basil
2 teaspoons chopped fresh thyme leaves
2 tablespoons chopped fresh Italian parsley
2 tablespoons chopped fresh celery leaves
4 tablespoons thinly sliced fresh basil, for serving

Place the barley in a stainless steel pan and add enough vegetable stock to cover. Set aside to soak for 4 hours.

In a large stockpot, heat the olive oil over medium heat. Add the garlic, onions and celery. Sauté for 3 to 5 minutes, or until just beginning to sweat.

Add the remaining vegetable stock and V8 juice and heat to a slow boil. Add the bay leaf and stock-soaked barley, bring to a simmer, cover, and cook for 30 minutes.

Add the salt, pepper and Tabasco, and stir gently. Add the remaining vegetables and simmer for 10 minutes. Then stir in the chopped basil, thyme, parsley and celery leaves.

Remove from the heat, let cool, and then refrigerate until needed.

To serve, reheat the soup to 165°F. Ladle the soup into bowls and top with the sliced basil.

Notes: More vegetable stock can be added to thin the soup if it becomes too thick.
This keeps in the fridge for a week and in the freezer for three months.

WINE:

Villa Maria, Sauvignon Blanc, "Lightly Sparkling," Marlborough, New Zealand 2010
Alternatives: *An aromatic, dry semi-sparkling wine. Italian "frizzante."*

TEXAS-STYLE STEAK CHILI
SERVES 4 TO 6

¼ cup canola oil

2½ pounds beef, cut into 1-by-¾-inch pieces – top round, sirloin or stew meat

4 cups diced white onions (¼-inch pieces)

1½ cups tomato sauce

¾ cup pineapple juice

1½ teaspoons red wine vinegar

¼ cup mild chili powder

1½ teaspoons ancho chili powder

¾ teaspoon chipotle chili powder (measure carefully: it's very spicy)

⅛ teaspoon habanero chili powder (measure carefully: it's very spicy)

2 teaspoons kosher salt

1 tablespoon plus 1 teaspoon sugar

¾ teaspoon ground dried basil

¾ teaspoon granulated garlic

¾ teaspoon sweet paprika

¾ teaspoon ground coriander

¾ teaspoon ground black pepper

¾ teaspoon ground cumin

3 bay leaves

For serving:
½ cup shredded Cheddar cheese
½ cup Crispy Tortilla Strips (page 112)
½ cup Fresh Tomato Salsa (page 85)
4 fresh cilantro sprigs

In a large stockpot or braising pan, heat the oil over medium-high heat. Add the beef and onions and sear until the onions are tender.

Add the remaining ingredients. Bring to a simmer, then lower the heat to medium-low or low, cover, and cook for 6 hours, stirring occasionally. This can also be cooked in a slow cooker at low temperature for 8 hours.

Serve immediately, or let cool and then refrigerate until needed. To reheat, place the chili in a double boiler (or slow cooker) and heat until the temperature is 165°F.

To serve, top with the shredded cheese, then the tortilla strips, salsa and cilantro sprigs.

WINE:
The "life is too short" pick:
Ruinart, Blanc de Blancs, Reims, Champagne, France
The "just because it's inexpensive doesn't mean you're cheap" pick:
Louis Bouillot, Crémant de Bourgogne, France
Alternatives: *Serious chili needs seriously delicious sparkling wine to balance the richness and heat. California sparkling wine or Italian Prosecco.*

VEGETABLE STOCK
MAKES 1 GALLON

¼ cup vegetable oil
1 cup peeled yellow onion cut in 1-inch pieces
1 cup leek cut in 1-inch pieces
1 cup celery cut in 1-inch pieces
½ cup cabbage cut in 1-inch pieces
1 cup peeled carrot cut in 1-inch pieces
½ cup peeled turnip cut in 1-inch pieces
1 cup peeled tomato cut in 1-inch pieces
2 tablespoons plus 2 teaspoons crushed whole garlic cloves
5 quarts cold water
1 teaspoon whole black peppercorns
1 teaspoon whole fennel seeds
4 whole cloves
4 bay leaves
4 fresh thyme sprigs
4 fresh Italian parsley sprigs

Heat the oil in a stockpot over medium-low heat. Add the vegetables, cover, and sweat for 10 to 12 minutes, stirring often to prevent browning.

Add the remaining ingredients to the pot. Bring to a boil, then reduce the heat to a simmer, cover, and cook for 40 minutes. Strain all the vegetables from the stock.

Cool the stock immediately in an ice bath. Store in the refrigerator until needed.

Note: When using the vegetable stock for your personal recipes, add salt to taste. When it is used in my recipes, salt is added in the individual recipes, so it does not have to be added here. This is a very complex and full-flavored vegetable stock, which can replace chicken stock in many recipes.

FISH STOCK
MAKES ½ GALLON

3 tablespoons olive oil
1 pound halibut bones and bodies, rinsed clean
1 cup peeled and coarsely diced yellow onion (¾- to 1-inch pieces)
½ cup peeled and coarsely diced carrots (¾- to 1-inch pieces)
½ cup coarsely diced celery (¾- to 1-inch pieces)
2 teaspoons minced fresh garlic
2 tablespoons minced shallot
3 cups Chablis or other dry white wine
¼ cup large fresh parsley sprigs
3 large fresh thyme sprigs
1 bay leaf
⅛ teaspoon cracked black peppercorns
10 cups cold water
¼ teaspoon kosher salt

Heat the oil in a large pot over medium-high heat. Add the fish bones and bodies, and cook for 6 to 8 minutes, or until the fish is broken up. Add the onions, carrots, celery, garlic and shallots. Sauté until the onions are translucent.

Continue to sauté, breaking the bodies down into smaller pieces with a metal kitchen spoon, until the fish bones are cooked through.

Add the remaining ingredients. Bring to a simmer, then reduce the heat to maintain a very low simmer. Cover and let simmer for 1½ hours, skimming periodically to remove any foam from the surface.

Strain the stock through a fine-mesh strainer. Then strain through a coffee filter to remove any sediment.

Let cool, then refrigerate until needed.

CLEAR CHICKEN STOCK
MAKES 1 GALLON

8 pounds chicken necks and backs, cut into 1- to 2-inch pieces
6 quarts cold water
1 cup peeled and coarsely chopped yellow onion (1-inch pieces)
½ cup coarsely chopped celery (1-inch pieces)
½ cup coarsely chopped carrots (1-inch pieces)
3 tablespoons crushed whole garlic cloves
1 teaspoon whole black peppercorns
2 bay leaves
1 teaspoon chopped fresh thyme leaves
2 tablespoons chopped fresh Italian parsley

Place the chicken necks and backs in a stockpot and cover with the water. Add the remaining ingredients. Bring to a boil, then reduce to a gentle simmer. Cook, uncovered, for 4 to 5 hours, skimming the top often.

Strain the stock.

Cool immediately in an ice bath. Refrigerate until needed.

VEAL BROWN STOCK
MAKES 1 GALLON

10 pounds veal bones, cut into pieces with the marrow exposed
2 gallons cold water, divided
8 ounces yellow onion, peeled and chopped into 1-inch pieces
4 ounces celery, cut into 1-inch pieces
4 ounces carrots, cut into 1-inch pieces
4 ounces tomato paste
1½ ounces whole garlic cloves, crushed
1 teaspoon whole black peppercorns
2 bay leaves
8 to 10 large fresh thyme sprigs
15 to 18 whole fresh Italian parsley sprigs

Preheat the oven to 375°F.

Rinse the bones and dry completely. Place in a roasting pan and roast in the oven for 60 to 90 minutes, or until they are a medium-dark caramel brown. Remove the bones from the pan. Reserve the pan.

Place the bones in a stockpot and add 1½ gallons of the water.

Place the onions, celery and carrots in the reserved roasting pan and set on the stovetop over medium heat. Add the tomato paste and cook until the mixture is a dark caramelized color, about 30 minutes. Be careful not to burn or char the bottom of the pan. Transfer the vegetables to the stockpot.

Add the garlic, peppercorns, bay leaves, thyme and parsley.

Add the remaining water to the roasting pan and stir to deglaze. Add to the stockpot. Let simmer, uncovered, over very low heat for 10 to 12 hours, skimming the top as needed.

Strain the stock.

Let cool, then store in the refrigerator until needed.

Notes: It is important to caramelize the bones and vegetables but not burn them. The stock should be slow-simmered, not boiled (boiling makes it cloudy). Last but not least, the stock should be skimmed often, at least 5 or 6 times during the simmering process.

Adriatic Grill is the Bill and Monique and John restaurant. We are here on site, but it wouldn't be here without John. It's a very interesting setup; it's not very common for two chefs to get together and do something like this. One thing I learned from my corporate life is that I'm an advocate for group brainstorming and consensus. Most chefs are about themselves, but I don't live in that world. This partnership is about the fact that he totally respects what Monique and I have done and he understands the pain we have gone through, and we totally respect what he has done. It wouldn't have worked with anybody else. He could have just come down here and changed stuff; instead he just said, you guys are on the right track, because we really believe in it. What I love about working with him is, there's always something that comes about to get us to the next step.

BILL TRUDNOWSKI
CHEF / PARTNER, ADRIATIC GRILL

We had to work to get him to trust us. We are here for the long haul, and he gets it. I had a car accident with the mini van, and the engine was done. No one was hurt, but everyone was upset. So it sat there for a year, and I took the bus to work with a baby. We had one car, so John called us and said, "I have a lead for you. Someone wants to give you a car." Here we had one car, and we were behind in those payments, too. We ended up losing that car, and John had someone who wanted to give us a car. He said, "Look at this station wagon online — you can get all the kids in it. Here is the VIN number you need to be in Seattle tomorrow and pick up this car." He asked, "Can Monique drive a stick?" Bill went up to Seattle and there was a car waiting for us. We asked him who did it and he wouldn't tell us.

MONIQUE TRUDNOWSKI
MANAGING PARTNER, ADRIATIC GRILL

SUSHI

SUSHI – MAKI-STYLE CALIFORNIA ROLL

SERVES 1

1 half sheet (cut lengthwise) of nori (dried seaweed)
¾ cup Sushi Rice (page 129)
1 teaspoon sesame seeds, toasted
2 ¹⁄₁₆ teaspoons wasabi paste, divided
½ teaspoon Japanese mayonnaise
2 avocado wedges (⅙ avocado)
1½ teaspoons tobiko (orange flying fish roe) or masago (capelin roe)
2 strips of English cucumber – 3 by ¼ by ¼ inches, skin on, soft center removed
2 tablespoons fresh Dungeness crab meat (about 1 ounce)
1 tablespoon sliced sweet pink pickled ginger (shoga)
Soy sauce, for serving

Special equipment: bamboo sushi mat; sushi knife (optional)

Clean your hands thoroughly before rolling sushi.

This roll is an inside-out style, with the rice on the outside of the roll.

Place the nori sheet, shiny side down, on a sushi mat. Spread the rice evenly over the whole sheet. Your fingers must be moist, not wet, to spread sushi rice; have a small dish of warm water to dip your fingers in. Sprinkle the toasted sesame seeds evenly over the rice. Cover the entire surface of the rice-covered nori sheet with a sheet of plastic wrap. Flip over so the plastic is now in contact with the sushi mat.

Spread ¹⁄₁₆ teaspoon of wasabi paste in a line across the center of the nori sheet. Spread the Japanese mayonnaise across the sheet beside the wasabi. Place the avocado, tobiko, cucumber and crab on top of the mayonnaise in a strip slightly off the center, toward the closest edge of the sheet.

Using the sushi mat, roll the rice-covered nori over the filling (see photo, page 127). Starting at the ends of the roll, use both thumbs and forefingers to press the roll together, continuing to press as you move toward the center of the roll. Move out to the end of the roll, and while holding the mat, press in any ingredients protruding from the ends.

Remove the mat, then lift the plastic and slowly move the plastic out while rolling the rice away from you.

Cut the sushi into 6 even pieces with a moistened sushi knife or very sharp slicing knife. Place the sushi pieces on a plate, side by side in 2 rows of 3. Garnish with a pyramid of wasabi paste and a pickled ginger roll. Serve with soy sauce.

SUSHI – MAKI-STYLE SPICY TUNA ROLL
SERVES 1

1 half sheet (cut lengthwise) of nori (dried seaweed)
¾ cup Sushi Rice (page 129)
2 ¹⁄₁₆ teaspoons wasabi paste, divided
2 tablespoons Spicy Tuna Mix
2 strips of English cucumber – 3 by ¼ by ¼ inch, skin on, soft center removed
1 tablespoon sliced sweet pink pickled ginger (shoga)
Soy sauce, for serving

SPICY TUNA MIX
MAKES 8 TABLESPOONS

6 tablespoons minced or ground fresh sashimi-grade ahi tuna
½ teaspoon togarashi seasoning (Japanese spice blend)
1 tablespoon Sriracha sauce (red chili sauce), preferably Shark brand
1½ teaspoons tobiko (orange flying fish roe)
1½ teaspoons thinly sliced green onion (⅛-inch pieces)
1½ teaspoons sesame seeds, toasted
1 teaspoon toasted sesame oil

Special equipment: bamboo sushi mat; sushi knife (optional)

Prepare the Spicy Tuna Mix: Combine all the ingredients and mix until blended. Refrigerate until needed. This can be made up to 4 hours before using, but for the best appearance, use immediately.

Clean your hands thoroughly before rolling sushi.

This roll is an inside-out style, with the rice on the outside of the roll.

Place the nori sheet, shiny side down, on the sushi mat. Spread the rice evenly over the whole sheet. Your fingers must be moist, not wet, to spread sushi rice; have a small dish of warm water to dip your fingers in. Cover the entire surface of the rice-covered nori sheet with a sheet of plastic wrap. Flip over so the plastic is now in contact with the sushi mat.

Spread ¹⁄₁₆ teaspoon of wasabi paste in a line across the center of the nori sheet. Place the spicy tuna mix and the cucumber slices on top of the wasabi.

Using the sushi mat, roll the rice-covered nori over the filling (see photo). Starting at the ends of the roll, use both thumbs and forefingers to press the roll together, continuing to press as you move toward the center of the roll. Move out to the end of the roll, and while holding the mat, press in any ingredients protruding from the ends.

Remove the mat, then lift the plastic and slowly move the plastic out while rolling the rice away from you.

Cut the sushi into 6 even pieces with a moistened sushi knife or very sharp slicing knife.

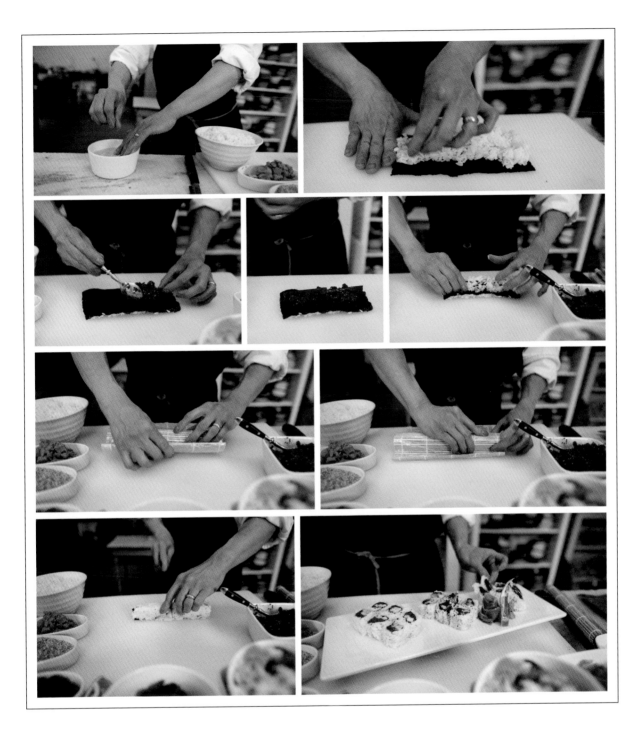

Place the sushi pieces on a plate, side by side
in 2 rows of 3. Garnish with a pyramid of
wasabi paste and a pickled ginger roll. Serve
with soy sauce.

SUSHI – MAKI-STYLE WASHINGTON ROLL
SERVES 1

1 half-sheet (cut lengthwise) of nori (dried seaweed)
¾ cup Sushi Rice
1 teaspoon sesame seeds, toasted
2 ¹⁄₁₆ teaspoons wasabi paste, divided
4 pieces peeled Granny Smith apple – 3 by ¼ by ¼ inch
1 tablespoon plus 1½ teaspoons chopped smoked salmon (¼-inch pieces)
1 tablespoon plus 1½ teaspoons Dungeness crab meat (about ¾ ounce)
1 tablespoon sliced sweet pink pickled ginger (shoga)
Soy sauce, for serving

Special equipment: bamboo sushi mat; sushi knife (optional)

Clean your hands thoroughly before rolling sushi.

This roll is an inside-out style, with the rice on the outside of the roll.

Place the nori sheet, shiny side down, on the sushi mat. Spread the rice evenly over the whole sheet. Your fingers must be moist, not wet, to spread sushi rice; have a small dish of warm water to dip your fingers in. Sprinkle the toasted sesame seeds evenly over the rice. Cover the entire surface of the rice-covered nori sheet with a sheet of plastic wrap. Flip over so the plastic is now in contact with the sushi mat.

Spread ¹⁄₁₆ teaspoon of wasabi paste in a line across the center of the nori sheet. Place the apple pieces end to end on the wasabi, then evenly distribute the smoked salmon and crab in a strip slightly off the center, next to the apples, toward the closest edge of the sheet.

Using the sushi mat, roll the rice-covered nori over the filling (see photo, page 127). Starting at the ends of the roll, use both thumbs and forefingers to press the roll together, continuing to press as you move to the center of the roll. Move out to the end of the roll, and while holding the mat, press in any ingredients protruding from the ends.

Remove the mat, then lift the plastic and slowly move the plastic out while rolling the rice away from you.

Cut the sushi into 6 even pieces with a moistened sushi knife or very sharp slicing knife. Place the sushi pieces on a plate, side by side in 2 rows of 3. Garnish with a pyramid of wasabi paste and a pickled ginger roll. Serve with soy sauce.

WINE:
  The "life is too short" pick:
  Rihaku, Sake, "Wandering Poet," Junmai Ginjo, Shimane, Japan
  The "just because it's inexpensive doesn't mean you're cheap" pick:
  Manotsuru, Sake, "Crane," Junmai, Sado Island, Japan
  Alternatives: *Crisp, clean, vinous-style sake that balances the multiple layers of flavors and textures of the rolls. Serve the sake slightly chilled.*

SUSHI RICE
MAKES 3 CUPS

1 cup Calrose medium- or short-grain round white rice
1 cup water

SUSHI RICE VINEGAR
1 tablespoon plus 2¼ teaspoons sugar
1 teaspoon kosher salt
3 tablespoons unseasoned rice vinegar (no more than 4.2% acidity), divided

Special equipment: rice cooker (optional); small electric fan (optional)

Prepare the Sushi Rice Vinegar: In a saucepan combine the sugar, salt and half the vinegar. Stir over medium-high heat until the sugar and salt have dissolved. Remove from the heat.

In a clean nonreactive container, combine the seasoned vinegar and the remaining vinegar. Let cool, then store, covered, at room temperature.

Soak the rice in a large bowl of cold water for 1 to 2 minutes. Transfer to a strainer, then lightly scrub the rice with your hands and rinse with cold water until the water runs clear.

Place the rice in the insert of the rice cooker with the water. Cover and start the cooking cycle. The rice should stay in the cooker for 35 minutes undisturbed. This includes a 15-minute period after the 20-minute cooking cycle is completed, during which time the rice should steep. (To cook the rice on a stovetop, place the rice and water in a saucepan. Bring to a boil, then lower the heat to a very low simmer, cover, and cook for 20 minutes. Remove from the heat and let sit, covered, for an additional 15 minutes.)

Immediately after completion of the 35-minute cook/steep cycle, transfer the rice to a large plastic bowl. While the rice is still warm, add the sushi vinegar. Stir the rice with either a wooden rice paddle or a rubber spatula with right and left slicing motions to separate the grains. The rice should be stirred constantly while you are adding the vinegar, then occasionally while it is cooling. While you are stirring to season and cool the rice, it should also be fanned — a small electric fan works well, or you can wave a piece of cardboard back and forth. This is an important step: fanning speeds the cooling process, preventing the rice from overcooking and becoming mushy, and it helps the rice develop a glossy sheen while absorbing the vinegar.

Do not refrigerate the rice. Store at room temperature in a nonreactive tub (covered with a plastic or wooden top) until it is ready to be used (within 4 hours).

Note: Sushi rice is the base for great sushi. In Japan, some sushi apprentices are trained and required to make rice for more than two years before they are allowed to touch the fish.

This recipe is simple and produces very nice sushi rice. The key is to not overcook the rice.

I got a call from this guy, John Howie. He left me a message saying, "Hi, I'm John Howie. I am opening a restaurant in Bellevue. Nancy Leson recommended I call you. Would you be interested?" This was about December 2001. I said, "No, no thanks." Who's John Howie and where's Bellevue? I really didn't know the Eastside. So I said no and he was persistent. He called me the next week and said, "I'd really just like to talk to you and tell you what we're doing." And I said, "No, I'm ready to put my roots down and stick around for a while."

A week later, I got a call up in my office: "There is a man downstairs that wants to talk with you." I got down there and I see this very large man who says, "Hi, I'm John Howie and I am not going to take no for an answer." I said, "Oh, really? OK." So we went to the coffee shop across the street and he gave me a blank piece of paper and said, "What is it you would like?" And so, for me mainly, number one was the quality of life, number two was some sort of partnership, and number three was a list of odds and ends that any wine dork wants in a restaurant. He said OK. If I am writing my own ticket, how can I not take that trip?

I didn't know what to think of John initially. I thought, he is obviously one who gets what he wants. I inquired around town about John Howie and got a sense of his reputation. And I was preparing myself for that. I had worked for some real Type A personalities before. John saw that I was really committed to his vision and to the restaurant and I stuck by him as well.

ERIK LIEDHOLM
PARTNER
COMPANY WINE DIRECTOR - ADVANCED SOMMELIER
JOHN HOWIE RESTAURANT GROUP

Fish & Shellfish

FISH WITH BLACK BEANS AND MANGO SALSA
SERVES 4

4 fish fillets, 6½ ounces each, ¾ inch thick, with no blood line – mahi mahi, spearfish, swordfish or
     other game fish
2 teaspoons Dry Jerk Seasoning (page 135), divided
3 cups Cilantro Rice, warm (page 88)
4 fresh cilantro sprigs

JERK MARINADE
1 tablespoon plus 1½ teaspoons Wet Jerk Seasoning (page 135)
3 tablespoons Pickapeppa sauce
1 tablespoon plus 1½ teaspoons fresh lime juice
½ cup plus 2 tablespoons canola oil

SPICY JAMAICAN BLACK BEANS
2 tablespoons clarified butter (page 135)
¼ cup diced white onion (¼-inch pieces)
¼ cup diced carrots (¼-inch pieces)
¼ cup diced celery (¼-inch pieces)
1½ teaspoons very finely minced fresh garlic
¼ cup tomato puree
4 cups Chicken Stock (page 120)
¾ cup dried black beans
2 tablespoons Pickapeppa sauce
⅜ teaspoon crushed red pepper flakes
⅜ teaspoon whole dried thyme
1 teaspoon Dry Jerk Seasoning (page 135)
¼ pound smoked ham hock (or ¼ cup diced cooked ham or bacon)
1 teaspoon kosher salt

This recipe calls for smoked ham hock. You could also substitute almost any regular ham as long as it is in a chunk.

MANGO SALSA
¾ cup diced fresh mango (¼-inch pieces)
2 tablespoons diced red onion (⅛-inch pieces)
1 teaspoon fresh lime juice
1 tablespoon fresh orange juice
½ teaspoon minced fresh orange zest
2 teaspoons coarsely chopped fresh cilantro
½ teaspoon seeded, finely minced habanero chile
½ teaspoon sugar

LIME CREAM
3 tablespoons sour cream
2 teaspoons whipping cream
2 teaspoons fresh lime juice
¼ teaspoon very finely minced fresh lime zest

Special equipment: squeeze bottle with a large tip

Prepare the Jerk Marinade: In a mixing bowl, combine the jerk seasoning, Pickapeppa and lime juice. Whip until well blended. Slowly add the oil with the mixer running at medium-high speed, until completely incorporated. Refrigerate until needed.

Prepare the Spicy Jamaican Black Beans: Heat the clarified butter in a soup pot over medium-high heat. Add the onions, carrots, celery and garlic. Sauté over medium heat for 3 to 4 minutes.

Add the remaining ingredients except the salt. Bring to a boil, then reduce the heat, cover, and slowly simmer for 1½ hours, or until the beans are tender, stirring occasionally.

Remove the ham hock, take the meat off the bone, mince very fine, and return to the pot. Skim any excess fatty liquids off the surface.

Strain the beans from the liquid. Puree half of the beans in a blender, adding as much liquid as necessary. Then combine the puree with the remaining beans and liquid, stirring to blend. Add the salt. Refrigerate until needed.

Prepare the Mango Salsa: Combine all the ingredients and mix until well blended. Refrigerate until needed.

Prepare the Lime Cream: Mix the sour cream and whipping cream together until loose and creamy. Stir in the lime juice and zest. Transfer to a squeeze bottle with a large tip and refrigerate until needed, up to 2 days.

Place the fish in a nonreactive dish and add ¾ cup of the marinade. Let marinate in the refrigerator for at least 6 hours and no more than 12 hours, turning at least once to ensure even marination. Remove from the marinade and refrigerate until needed.

Preheat the grill or a grill pan to medium-high.

Place the fish on the grill and baste with some of the remaining marinade. Then season with a third of the dry jerk seasoning blend. Grill until marks are formed, about 1½ minutes, then change the angle on the grill to create diamond marks and grill for 1½ minutes. Turn the fish over, baste with marinade, and season with another third of the dry jerk seasoning. Grill for 1½ minutes, then change the angle and grill for another 1½ minutes, or until the internal temperature is 110-120°F. Baste one last time with the marinade and season with the remaining dry jerk seasoning.

To serve, place some rice on each plate on the upper right side from 1 o'clock to 3 o'clock. Then place the heated beans around the exterior of the rice from 12 o'clock to 4 o'clock, spreading over the entire open area of the plate.

Place the fish slightly overlapping the rice and beans at around 4 to 5 o'clock. Place the salsa on the top end of the fish, cascading onto the rice around the 12 o'clock position.

Starting at the 10 o'clock position in the beans, squeeze a 1-teaspoon-size drop of Lime Cream, then add 4 increasingly smaller drops along the beans, ending with a ¼-teaspoon drop at the bottom of the plate.

Garnish with a fresh cilantro sprig at the top of the fish and salsa.

Note: Quality dry jerk and wet jerk seasonings can be purchased. I recommend the Busha Browne brand.

WET JERK SEASONING
MAKES 2½ CUPS

2 cups minced green onions – both green
    and white parts
2 tablespoons minced fresh habanero or Scotch
    bonnet chile
2 tablespoons dried whole thyme leaves
2 teaspoons ground black pepper
1 tablespoon plus 2 teaspoons kosher salt
1 tablespoon ground allspice
1 teaspoon ground nutmeg
¼ teaspoon sugar
2 teaspoons fresh lemon juice
¾ cup water

In a food processor, combine the green onions,
chile and thyme. Pulse until blended and the
thyme is chopped.

Transfer to a saucepan and add all the
remaining ingredients. Bring to a boil, then
reduce the heat to very low. Cover the pot
tightly and cook, removing the lid and stirring
every 5 minutes, until the water is 85 percent
gone. This will take approximately 45 to 60
minutes.

Let cool, then refrigerate in an airtight container
for up to 6 months. (If you drizzle olive oil over
the top, this will last for up to a year.)

DRY JERK SEASONING
MAKES 7 TABLESPOONS

1 teaspoon ground dried habanero or Scotch
    bonnet chile
2 tablespoons granulated onion
1 tablespoon plus ½ teaspoon dried whole
    thyme leaves
1 tablespoon dried sliced chives
1 teaspoon coarsely ground black pepper
2 teaspoons kosher salt
2 teaspoons ground allspice
½ teaspoon ground nutmeg
½ teaspoon ground cinnamon
¼ teaspoon ground cloves
¼ teaspoon granulated garlic
1 teaspoon packed light brown sugar

Combine all the ingredients in a spice grinder.
Pulse 3 to 4 times.

Store in an airtight container at room
temperature.

CLARIFIED BUTTER

Clarified butter is made by melting unsalted
butter over low heat and then removing
both the foam that comes to the top and the
milky residue (whey) that sits on the bottom.
The remaining golden oil is clarified butter.
Clarified butter can be chilled and kept in the
refrigerator for up to two months. Ghee is a
clarified butter product that can be purchased.

WINE:
    The "life is too short" pick:
    Peter Michael, "L'Après-Midi," Knights Valley, Sonoma County, California 2009
    The "just because it's inexpensive doesn't mean you're cheap" pick:
    Chinook, Semillon, Yakima Valley, Washington 2009
    Alternatives: *A white with ripe pear and tropical fruit and a touch of oak. French Sauvignon/Semillon*
        blend (Bordeaux Blanc).

POTATO CHIP–CRUSTED HALIBUT

SERVES 4

4 halibut pieces, 6 ounces each, 3-by-4-inch block cut, 1½ inches thick, skin off

1¼ teaspoons sea salt, divided

¾ teaspoon ground black pepper

¾ cup crushed Tim's potato chips (⅛- to ¼-inch pieces)

½ cup haricot verts, stems removed, blanched until tender in boiling water for 1 to 2 minutes, then chilled

¼ cup peeled and thinly sliced watermelon radish (1/16 inch thick)

2 cups fresh baby arugula

¼ cup thinly sliced red onion (1/16-by-½-inch slices)

¼ cup Lemon-Thyme Vinaigrette (page 62), divided

1 large heirloom tomato, approximately 4-inch diameter, room temperature, cut into eight ¼-inch-thick slices

Preheat the oven to 400°F.

Season the halibut with 1 teaspoon salt and the pepper. Roll in the potato chips, coating on all sides and packing a little extra on top of the fish. Place the fish on a baking sheet and bake for 10 to 13 minutes, depending on how thick the pieces are.

Meanwhile, place the haricot verts, radishes, arugula and onion in a salad bowl. Toss with 3 tablespoons of the vinaigrette.

Place 2 tomato slices on the upper right edge of each plate, leaving ½ inch of space to the edge. Season the tomatoes with the remaining ¼ teaspoon salt. Next, add the vegetable salad, slightly overlapping the tomato slices and cascading down the plate.

Remove the fish from the oven and place on the plates, slightly propped up on the salad mix. Drizzle the remaining vinaigrette around the front of each plate and over the salad.

Notes:

Watermelon radishes are available only from midsummer to early fall. You can use other varieties as a substitute.

Heirloom tomatoes come in many different colors and sizes. For this dish, you want a large beefsteak-style heirloom tomato. Using different colors (yellow, green, orange or red) adds to the appearance of the dish.

WINE:

The "life is too short" pick:

Inama, Soave, Vigneto du Lot, Veneto, Italy 2008

The "just because it's inexpensive doesn't mean you're cheap" pick:

Feudi di San Gregorio, Falanghina, Campania, Italy 2009

Alternatives: *A white wine that has balance between bracing acidity and rich fruit. Spanish Albariño or dry Oregon Pinot Gris.*

PARMIGIANO-CRUSTED HALIBUT

SERVES 4

1 large egg
⅓ cup milk
½ cup finely grated Parmigiano-Reggiano cheese
¼ cup finely grated Asiago cheese
¼ cup finely crushed panko bread crumbs
8 halibut medallions, ⅜ to ½ inch thick, 2½ to 3 ounces each
½ teaspoon salt
½ teaspoon freshly ground pepper
2 tablespoons clarified butter (page 135)
1 tablespoon Lemon-Chive Oil (page 62)
4 fresh chervil sprigs

CREAMY BUTTER SAUCE
1 tablespoon whipping cream
2 tablespoons salted butter
2 tablespoons unsalted butter

Prepare the Creamy Butter Sauce: Place the cream in a saucepan and warm over medium heat. Gradually add the butter to the cream until it is all melted (if the sauce is too thick at this point, slowly stir in some warm water to thin to the proper consistency). Keep warm until needed.

To prepare the halibut, mix the egg and milk together until blended. Set aside.

In a food processor, blend the cheeses and bread crumbs until powdered. Transfer to a shallow bowl.

Season the fish medallions evenly with the salt and pepper. Then dip them in the egg wash and press into the cheese mixture. Refrigerate until needed.

Preheat a flat-top grill or nonstick sauté pan over medium-high heat. Add the clarified butter. Add the fish and cook for 1½ minutes on one side, or until the topping is golden brown around the edges. Turn and cook for 1 minute on the other side, or until the internal temperature is 120°F.

Remove the fish from the grill or pan and place 2 pieces, slightly overlapping, on each plate. Pour the Creamy Butter Sauce over the fish. Place dots of the Lemon-Chive Oil around the plate. Garnish with the chervil sprigs.

WINE:
The "life is too short" pick:
Arnaud Ente, Meursault, "Clos des Ambres," Burgundy, France 2007
The "just because it's inexpensive doesn't mean you're cheap" pick:
Talbott, Chardonnay, "Kali Hart," Monterey, California 2009
Alternatives: *A rich white with bracing acidity and a bit of toasty oak. Washington Chardonnay.*

Halibut Puttanesca with Olive Tapenade
Serves 4

4 halibut pieces, 6 ounces each, 3-by-4-inch block cut, 1½ inches thick, skin off
1½ teaspoons Seafood Seasoning Blend
2 tablespoons olive oil
12 ounces Potato Gnocchi (page 92), or purchased
¼ cup Kalamata Olive Tapenade
4 fresh Italian parsley sprigs

Puttanesca Sauce

3 tablespoons olive oil
1 tablespoon plus 1 teaspoon shaved garlic slices
6 tablespoons diced white onion (¼-inch pieces)
1 tablespoon plus 1 teaspoon capers, drained
2 teaspoons very finely minced high-quality cured anchovy
2 tablespoons coarsely chopped Kalamata olives
2 cups canned pear tomatoes in juice, crushed into ¼- to ½-inch pieces
⅛ teaspoon crushed red pepper flakes
¼ teaspoon kosher salt
2 tablespoons very thinly sliced fresh basil

Prepare the Puttanesca Sauce: Place the olive oil and garlic in a saucepan over medium heat and sauté until tender. Add the onion and sauté until tender.

Add the capers, anchovies, olives, tomatoes and red pepper. Simmer for 10 to 15 minutes, or until the sauce reduces slightly and thickens. Remove from the heat and let cool.

Stir in the salt and then fold in the basil. Refrigerate until needed.

Preheat the oven to 425°F.

Season the halibut with the seafood seasoning blend. Place the olive oil in a large ovenproof sauté pan over medium heat. When the pan is hot, add the halibut and sear on one side until there is a golden brown crust. Turn the fish over, then transfer to the oven until just done, approximately 6 to 8 minutes or an internal temperature of 120°F.

Meanwhile, place the gnocchi in boiling water and cook until tender, approximately 2 to 3 minutes. When cooked completely, the gnocchi will float.

Place the puttanesca sauce in a sauté pan and begin to heat. Add the gnocchi and toss until completely coated. Place in pasta bowls, mounded high in the center.

Remove the halibut from the oven and set on top of the gnocchi in the bowls. Place a dollop of tapenade on the center of each fillet. Garnish with parsley sprigs.

KALAMATA OLIVE TAPENADE
MAKES ½ CUP

¼ teaspoon very finely minced fresh garlic
⅜ cup coarsely chopped Kalamata olives
1 teaspoon finely minced anchovy
1 teaspoon capers, drained and excess liquid squeezed out
⅛ teaspoon chopped fresh thyme leaves
⅛ teaspoon very finely chopped fresh rosemary
⅛ teaspoon kosher salt
1½ teaspoons fresh lemon juice
1 tablespoon extra-virgin olive oil

Place all the ingredients in a small food processor and pulse until coarsely pureed. Refrigerate until needed.

SEAFOOD SEASONING BLEND
MAKES 1 CUP

¾ cup Diamond kosher salt
2 tablespoons coarsely ground black pepper
2 tablespoons granulated onion

Combine all the ingredients and mix well.

Store in an airtight container at room temperature for up to 6 months. If the mixture cakes, that's okay — just break it up with your fingers.

WINE:
The "life is too short" pick:
Château de Fonsalette, Côtes du Rhône, Reserve, Rhône, France 2007
The "just because it's inexpensive doesn't mean you're cheap" pick:
d'Arenberg, Grenache, "The Derelict," McLaren Vale, Australia 2007
Alternatives: *A red with moderate tannin and white-pepper, earthy notes and high-toned fruit. Washington State Grenache.*

HALIBUT WITH CHANTERELLE SUCCOTASH AND BACON
SERVES 4

4 halibut pieces, 5 ounces each, 3-by-4-inch block cut, 1½ inches thick, skin off
2 tablespoons clarified butter (page 135)
1½ teaspoons sea salt, divided
½ teaspoon freshly ground black pepper
¼ cup semicrisp-cooked ¼-inch bacon slices (about ½ cup raw), grease reserved
        (see note)
6 tablespoons unsalted butter
1 tablespoon plus 1 teaspoon minced shallots
¼ cup Vegetable Stock (page 118)
¼ cup whipping cream
1 teaspoon sliced chives (⅛-inch pieces)

CARAMELIZED ONION RELISH
1 tablespoon bacon grease
⅔ cup julienne-sliced sweet white onion (⅛ by 1 to 2 inches)
1 teaspoon packed light brown sugar
1 teaspoon cider vinegar

CHANTERELLE SUCCOTASH MIX
¾ cup fresh corn kernels (or thawed frozen corn; do not use canned)
½ cup coarsely chopped chanterelle mushrooms (¼- to ½-inch pieces)
½ cup edamame beans, fresh or thawed frozen
¼ cup diced red bell pepper (¼-inch pieces)

Prepare the Caramelized Onion Relish: Place the bacon grease in a sauté pan over medium heat. Add the onions and cook until lightly caramelized. Stir in the brown sugar and cook until dissolved.

Add the vinegar, remove from the heat, and let cool to room temperature. Refrigerate until needed.

Prepare the Chanterelle Succotash Mix: Combine all the ingredients and mix until well blended. Refrigerate until needed.

Preheat the oven to 350°F.

Brush the halibut with the clarified butter. Season with 1 teaspoon salt and the pepper.

Preheat a large ovenproof sauté pan over medium-high heat. Add the halibut and sear until the edges are golden brown. Turn the fish over and transfer the pan to the oven. Roast for 5 to 6 minutes, or until the internal temperature is approximately 120°F. Remove from the oven and let rest for 1 minute.

Place the onion relish and bacon — separated — on a sizzle platter or in an ovenproof sauté pan and place in the 350°F oven. Heat until the bacon is sizzling. (Mixing the bacon and onion before placing in the oven will prevent the bacon from crisping.)

Meanwhile, place the unsalted butter and shallots in a sauté pan and begin to heat over medium-high heat. Add the succotash mix and cook for 2 minutes. Add the vegetable stock, stirring to deglaze the pan, and let it reduce slightly (2 minutes). Add the cream and ½ teaspoon salt. Reduce again for 2 to 3 minutes, allowing the sauce to thicken (if you are using frozen corn rather than fresh, this may take longer). Divide the succotash mixture evenly among 4 large bowls.

Place the halibut on top of the succotash. Remove the onion relish and bacon from the oven and stir them together. Place the mixture on top of the halibut. Garnish with the chives.

Note: The bacon can be precooked to medium-crisp in a sauté pan or baked in the oven on a cookie sheet, then sliced for this recipe. Remember to save the bacon grease for the Caramelized Onion Relish.

WINE:
The "life is too short" pick:
Leeuwin, Chardonnay, "Art Series," Margaret River Valley, Australia 2007
The "just because it's inexpensive doesn't mean you're cheap" pick:
Chateau St. Jean, Chardonnay, "Robert Young Vineyard," Alexander Valley, California 2007
Alternatives: *A big, rich white wine with oak, butterscotch and caramelized apple that can stand up to the richness of the relish. French Chardonnay (Burgundy).*

HALIBUT WITH ASPARAGUS PROVENÇAL
SERVES 4

4 halibut pieces, 6 ounces each, 3-by-4-inch block cut, 1½ inches thick, skin off
    (this recipe also works well with sea bass, ono and Gulf snapper)
1 tablespoon plus 1 teaspoon sea salt, divided
2 teaspoons coarsely ground fresh pepper, divided
½ cup olive oil
2 tablespoons garlic shaved very thin in whole slices
    (with a Japanese mandoline or by hand)
½ cup minced white onion (⅛-inch pieces)
3 cups diced Roma (or heirloom) tomatoes (½-inch pieces)
2 to 2½ pounds asparagus, using only the top 4 inches of each
    spear, to yield 1 pound
4 fresh Italian parsley sprigs

GARLIC-LEMON OIL
2 tablespoons olive oil
2 teaspoons very finely minced fresh garlic
2 teaspoons very finely minced lemon zest
2 teaspoons fresh lemon juice

Asparagus comes in all sizes — from pencil thick to cigar thick. When determining where to cut your asparagus, it is best to pull out one piece from the bunch, hold both ends, and bend until it snaps. Where it snaps is where you should cut the rest of the asparagus. The bottom end of the spear is woody and usable only in stock. On larger asparagus, the stalk may still be slightly woody, so it should be peeled approximately two inches up from where it snapped.

Prepare the Garlic-Lemon Oil: Mix all the ingredients together. Refrigerate until needed.

Preheat the oven to 400°F.

Heat a large ovenproof sauté pan over medium-high heat.

Brush one side of the fish with one-third of the garlic-lemon oil. Season each piece of fish with ⅛ teaspoon of the salt and pepper. Place the fish, oiled side down, in the hot pan. Brush the other side of the fish with one-third of the garlic-lemon oil and then season each piece with ⅛ teaspoon of salt and pepper. Cook for 1 to 2 minutes, or until the fish is lightly browned around the edges. Turn the fish over and then transfer the pan to the oven and roast for 6 to 8 minutes, or until the internal temperature is 120°F. Remove from the oven and baste with the remaining garlic-lemon oil. Season each fillet with ⅛ teaspoon salt.

Meanwhile heat the olive oil in a sauté pan over high heat. When the oil is hot but not smoking, add the garlic and onion. Sauté until the garlic is turning golden brown. Toss lightly, then add the tomatoes and the remaining salt and pepper. Cook and toss until the tomatoes have softened.

Bring a pot of water to a boil. Add the asparagus. Cook pencil-size asparagus for 1½ to 2 minutes, or until al dente (adjust the cooking time for larger spears). Remove the asparagus from the boiling water, drain, and add to the sauté pan. Toss to coat the asparagus.

Place the asparagus on 4 plates with the spears pointing out to the edges of the plates, from 9 o'clock to 2 o'clock. Let some of the tomato, garlic and onion cling to the asparagus. The asparagus should be mounded 2 to 3 stalks high.

Place the halibut over the ends of the asparagus in the center of the plate. Place the remaining tomato, garlic and onion mixture on the top edge of the fish where it overlaps the asparagus. Garnish with parsley sprigs.

WINE:
The "life is too short" pick:
Domaine Tempier, Rosé, Bandol, France 2010
The "just because it's inexpensive doesn't mean you're cheap" pick:
Château d'Esclans, Rosé, "Whispering Angel," Provence, France 2010
Alternatives: *Virtually any Rosé (not white Zinfandel) that has been produced within one vintage of the current year.*

Mahi Mahi with Cilantro Rice and Avocado-Tomatillo Salsa

Serves 4

4 mahi mahi fillets, 6 ounces each, ¾ to 1 inch thick
1 teaspoon sea salt, divided
½ teaspoon freshly ground black pepper, divided
3 cups Cilantro Rice, warm (page 88)
4 lime slices – ½-inch-thick half-moons
4 large fresh cilantro sprigs

Spicy Black Beans

⅔ cup (6 ounces) dried black beans
1 small dried chipotle pepper
1 teaspoon coriander seeds
½ teaspoon cumin seeds
1 tablespoon canola oil
⅓ cup diced white onion (¼-inch pieces)
½ cup diced ripe tomatillos (½-inch pieces)
2 tablespoons charred, seeded, peeled and
    diced poblano chile (½-inch pieces)
2 teaspoons minced fresh garlic
2¾ cups Chicken Stock (page 120)
1 bay leaf
1 tablespoon plus 1½ teaspoons red wine
    vinegar
¾ teaspoon whole dried oregano
1 tablespoon water
1 tablespoon arrowroot or cornstarch
½ teaspoon ancho chili powder
⅛ teaspoon ground allspice
⅛ teaspoon ground black pepper
1/16 teaspoon habanero chili powder
1½ teaspoons kosher salt
2 tablespoons fresh lime juice
1 tablespoon roughly chopped fresh cilantro

Chili-Garlic Oil

1 tablespoon plus 1½ teaspoons olive oil
1½ teaspoons very finely minced fresh garlic
¾ teaspoon ancho chili powder
¾ teaspoon ground smoked paprika
¼ teaspoon chipotle chili powder
¼ teaspoon packed light brown sugar

Avocado-Tomatillo Salsa

¼ cup diced white onion (⅛-inch pieces)
2 tablespoons diced seeded Roma tomato
    (¼-inch pieces)
½ cup diced ripe tomatillo
    (¼-inch pieces) (see note)
1½ teaspoons fresh lime juice
1 tablespoon coarsely chopped fresh cilantro
½ teaspoon sea salt
1½ teaspoons olive oil
1 firm but ripe Hass avocado,
    cut in ½-inch dice

Prepare the Spicy Black Beans: Soak the black beans in 2 cups water overnight.

Heat a dry saucepan over medium heat. Add the chipotle, coriander and cumin, and toast until the fragrance of the ingredients is evident. Do not burn.

Add the oil and onion. Lower the heat to medium-low and cook until the onion is tender. Add the tomatillo, poblano and garlic, and sauté for 3 to 4 minutes.

Drain the black beans and add to the pot, along with the chicken stock, bay leaf, vinegar and oregano. Bring to a simmer, then reduce the heat to a slow simmer, cover, and cook until the beans are tender, approximately 30 minutes.

Meanwhile, combine the water and arrowroot, stirring until blended. Add to the beans, stir, and cook until the mixture thickens. Reduce, if necessary, until the mixture has a rich soupy consistency. Stir in the remaining ingredients.

Remove the chipotle pepper and puree in a small food processor with some of the liquid from the beans. Stir the puree into the beans. Remove from the heat and let cool. Refrigerate until needed.

Prepare the Chili-Garlic Oil: Combine all the ingredients in a blender and process for 1 minute, until thoroughly mixed. Set aside at room temperature.

Prepare the Avocado-Tomatillo Salsa: Combine all the ingredients except the avocado. Stir until well coated. Just before serving, gently stir in the avocado. Don't overmix, or the avocado will become mushy.

Note: Tomatillos look like green tomatoes with a thin paper husk. Ripe tomatillos should be fairly firm but still pliable to the touch. Remove the husk before using.

To prepare the fish, preheat the grill or grill pan to medium-high. Brush the mahi mahi with a third of the chili-garlic oil. Season with half of the salt and pepper.

Place the fish on the grill and cook for 1½ minutes. Change the angle of the fillets to create a diamond pattern and cook for 2 minutes. Turn the fillets over, baste with another third of the chili-garlic oil, and cook for 2½ minutes. Turn the fillets to a different angle and continue to cook until the internal temperature is 120-125°F.

Just before removing from the grill, baste the fish with the remaining chili-garlic oil and season with the remaining salt and pepper.

Meanwhile, reheat the black beans in a sauté pan.

Place some rice in the back center of each plate, leaving some open space behind it. Place the black beans around the front of the rice; some of the beans and sauce may spread around the back of the rice.

Place the grilled fish against the front side of the rice. Ladle the salsa on the top end of the fish, with some of it cascading down the back side of the rice. Garnish with lime slices and cilantro sprigs.

WINE:
   The "life is too short" pick:
   Josmeyer, Riesling, "The Dragon," Alsace, France 2009
   The "just because it's inexpensive doesn't mean you're cheap" pick:
   Chateau Ste. Michelle, Riesling, Washington 2010
   Alternatives: *A rich, slightly off-dry (semi-sweet) white wine with aromas and flavors of white flowers and pears. French Chenin Blanc (Vouvray/Montlouis).*

Mahi Mahi with Pineapple-Pomegranate Relish
Serves 4

8 mahi mahi medallions, 3½ ounces each, ½ inch thick, 3 by 4 inches
2 tablespoons clarified butter (page 135)
3 cups Citrus Rice, warmed (page 89)
½ cup Beurre Blanc (page 84)
¼ cup pomegranate molasses
12 small fresh cilantro sprigs

Aromatic Spice Crust
1½ teaspoons cumin seeds
1½ teaspoons coriander seeds
⅛ teaspoon ground cloves
⅜ teaspoon ground allspice
1 teaspoon coarsely ground black pepper
1½ teaspoons kosher salt

Pineapple-Pomegranate Relish
1 cup diced fresh pineapple (¼-inch pieces)
¼ cup fresh pomegranate seeds
2 tablespoons minced white onion
      (⅛-inch pieces)
¾ teaspoon finely minced fresh lemon zest
¼ teaspoon seeded and minced green jalapeño
1 tablespoon chopped fresh cilantro
¼ teaspoon kosher salt
1½ teaspoons packed light brown sugar

Prepare the Aromatic Spice Crust: Preheat a small dry sauté pan over medium heat. Add the cumin and coriander, and toast until light golden in color and the aroma fills the room. Let cool to room temperature.

Combine all the ingredients in a spice grinder and process to a fine mince. Store in an airtight container at room temperature.

Prepare the Pineapple-Pomegranate Relish: In a bowl, combine all the ingredients and mix until well blended. Refrigerate until needed. This can be made up to 24 hours in advance.

To cook the fish, preheat a large sauté pan over medium-high heat. Brush the medallions with the clarified butter, then season each medallion evenly with the spice crust. Place in the pan and sear for approximately 1½ to 2 minutes on each side, or until golden brown, with an internal temperature of 110-120°F.

Meanwhile, evenly distribute the rice and mound in the center of each plate. Remove the medallions from the pan and place overlapping on top of the rice.

Drizzle the warm Beurre Blanc around the outside of the rice, with a little over the top of the medallions. Then drizzle the pomegranate molasses around the rice on the sauce. Top the medallions with the relish, letting some cascade down the sides. Garnish with cilantro sprigs in the sauces surrounding the rice.

Wine:
The "life is too short" pick:
Kongsgaard, Chardonnay, Napa Valley, California 2007
The "just because it's inexpensive doesn't mean you're cheap" pick:
Columbia Crest, Chardonnay, "Grand Estates," Columbia Valley, Washington 2009
Alternatives: *A white wine with rich tropical fruit notes, vibrant acidity and toasty baking spice notes. French Chardonnay (Burgundy).*

BLACK COD WITH GINGER
SERVES 4

Black cod, also known as sablefish, can be difficult to find and expensive. You can substitute sea bass or even halibut for this recipe. It is preferable to use fresh fish, but if you must use frozen, prepare additional marinade, as the fish will release more moisture and so may not caramelize.

4 black cod fillets, 6 to 7 ounces each, 3 inches thick, skin on
¼ cup daikon or other radish sprouts
½ cup sliced sweet pickled ginger (shoga), rolled into 4 rose shapes

GINGER-MIRIN MARINADE
1 cup Aji mirin
1 tablespoon soy sauce
1 tablespoon minced peeled fresh ginger
1 tablespoon finely minced green onion
1 teaspoon finely minced fresh garlic
2 tablespoons sugar
1 teaspoon toasted sesame oil

Prepare the marinade: Combine all the ingredients and mix until the sugar has dissolved.

Pour the marinade into a glass or nonreactive dish. Add the fish, making sure it is completely covered with marinade. Cover and place in the refrigerator. Marinate for at least 12 hours and up to 24 hours, turning the fish two to three times to ensure even marination. Remove the fish from the marinade and refrigerate until needed. Reserve the marinade.

Preheat the oven to 500°F.

Place the fish in a large baking dish and top with ½ cup of the marinade. Set in the oven and cook for 8 to 10 minutes, or until the sauce is caramelizing and bubbling and the edges of the fish are caramelized. If there is no caramelization, place the fish under the broiler for 30 seconds to achieve some caramelization without overcooking the fish.

Remove the fish from the dish and place on plates, pouring any excess caramelized sauce over the fish. At the top of the fish, garnish with the daikon sprouts and ginger roses.

WINE:
The "life is too short" pick:
Domaine Zind-Humbrecht, Gewürztraminer, "Clos Windsbuhl," Alsace, France 2009
The "just because it's inexpensive doesn't mean you're cheap" pick:
Navarro, Gewürztraminer, Anderson Valley, California 2010
Alternatives: *A crisp yet off-dry white loaded with succulent stone fruit, white flowers and spice.*
Washington Viognier or French Viognier (Condrieu).

SEARED FISH WITH CUCUMBER-MACADAMIA NUT RELISH
SERVES 4

8 fish medallions, 3½ ounces each, ½ inch thick,
　　3 by 4 inches, skin off – escolar, halibut,
　　mahi mahi, Gulf snapper or similar variety
¾ teaspoon sea salt
¼ teaspoon freshly ground pepper
¼ cup vegetable or canola oil
14 snow peas, stems removed, halved diagonally
　　lengthwise
1½ pounds cooked sticky white rice
¾ cup Beurre Blanc (page 84)
¾ cup Mae Ploy Thai sweet chili sauce
4 large fresh cilantro sprigs

CUCUMBER-MACADAMIA NUT RELISH
1½ teaspoons sugar
1 tablespoon rice vinegar
¾ cup diced English cucumber, skin on
　　(¼-inch pieces) (see note)
¼ cup chopped toasted macadamia nuts
1 tablespoon coarsely chopped fresh cilantro
1 tablespoon Thai sweet chili sauce

SATEH MARINADE
¾ cup canola oil
3 tablespoons very finely minced fresh
　　lemongrass, light-colored stem only
1 tablespoon very finely minced fresh garlic
1 tablespoon Thai or Malaysian yellow curry
　　powder (Indian can be substituted)
1 tablespoon sugar
1 tablespoon Thai yellow curry paste
1 teaspoon Thai fish sauce

Prepare the Cucumber-Macadamia Nut Relish:
In a bowl, dissolve the sugar in the rice vinegar.

Add the cucumber and toss until well coated.
Let marinate for 30 minutes. Drain completely.

Add the macadamia nuts, cilantro and chili
sauce, and mix well. Refrigerate until needed.

Prepare the Sateh Marinade: Combine all the
ingredients in a food processor and pulse until
very finely minced. Refrigerate until needed.

Cover the fish medallions with the marinade,
and let marinate for 20 to 30 minutes. Remove
any excess marinade and season each medallion
evenly with the salt and pepper.

Preheat the grill or a sauté pan to medium-high.

Add the oil to the hot grill or sauté pan. Add the
medallions and sear for 2 to 3 minutes, until
the edges are lightly golden brown. Turn over
and sear the other side for 1 to 2 minutes.

Meanwhile, place the snow peas in boiling
water for 30 to 45 seconds. Drain.

To serve, place the snow peas around the outside edge of each plate, pointed side out. Place
the rice in the center of the plate overlapping
the ends of the snow peas. Drizzle the beurre
blanc and chili sauce over the peas and rice.

Remove the fish from the grill and stack on the
rice. Top the fish medallions with the relish.
Garnish with cilantro sprigs.

Note: English cucumber has no evident seeds. If English
cucumber is not available, the cucumber should be seeded.

WINE:
　　The "life is too short" pick:
　　Knoll, Grüner Veltliner, Smaragd, Ried Schütt, Wachau, Austria 2008
　　The "just because it's inexpensive doesn't mean you're cheap" pick:
　　Zocker, Grüner Veltliner, Paragon Vineyard, Edna Valley, California 2009
　　Alternatives: *A clean and dry yet rich white with candied vegetable notes. Spanish Albariño or French
　　　　Rhône blend (white).*

Ancho Chili–Rubbed Salmon with Sweet Chili Hollandaise

Serves 4

4 salmon pieces, 6 to 7 ounces each, block cut, skin off
1 teaspoon canola oil
Southwestern Roasted Corn Mashed Potatoes (page 98), for serving
4 fresh cilantro sprigs

Ancho Chili Rub

2 teaspoons packed light brown sugar
1 teaspoon kosher salt
1/16 teaspoon chipotle chili powder
1½ teaspoons mild chili powder blend
3/16 teaspoon dry mustard
¼ teaspoon paprika
1 teaspoon ancho chili powder

Lime Cream

1 tablespoon plus 1½ teaspoons sour cream
1 teaspoon fresh lime juice
½ teaspoon minced fresh lime zest

BBQ Base

¾ teaspoon olive oil
1 tablespoon plus 1½ teaspoons very finely minced onion
¾ teaspoon ancho chili powder
1/16 teaspoon chipotle chili powder
3/8 teaspoon mild chili powder blend
1½ teaspoons balsamic vinegar
¾ teaspoon Dijon mustard
1 teaspoon light brown sugar
1 tablespoon molasses
¼ teaspoon Worcestershire sauce
¼ teaspoon minced fresh garlic
2 tablespoons tomato paste

Sweet Chili Hollandaise

2 large egg yolks
1½ teaspoons fresh lemon juice
1½ teaspoons dry white wine
4 tablespoons cold salted butter, cut into 4 even chunks
Dash of Tabasco sauce
2 tablespoons BBQ Base
3/8 teaspoon ancho chili powder

Prepare the Ancho Chili Rub: Combine all the ingredients and mix until well blended. Store in an airtight container.

Rub the fish with the ancho chili rub. Let sit for 2 to 3 hours, uncovered, in the refrigerator. This will allow the dry rub to penetrate the salmon. (If desired, place the salmon in a smoker and cold-smoke for 15 minutes. This will add a smoky richness to the fish. But it can be prepared without it.)

Prepare the Lime Cream: Combine all the ingredients and stir until blended. Refrigerate until needed.

Prepare the BBQ Base: Heat the olive oil in a saucepan over medium heat. Add the onion and chili powders, and sauté until the onion is soft and translucent. Add the vinegar and stir to deglaze the pan. Add the remaining ingredients, bring to a simmer, then reduce the heat to very low and simmer for 2 to 3 minutes. Let cool, then store in the refrigerator.

Prepare the Sweet Chili Hollandaise: Whisk the egg yolks, lemon juice and wine in a stainless steel or copper bowl over gently simmering water in a double boiler. Continue whisking constantly. When it just begins to warm, add the butter 1 piece at a time and whisk until melted. Continue to cook, whisking constantly, until the mixture has a thick ribbon consistency. Remove from the heat. Stir in the Tabasco, BBQ Base and ancho powder. Keep warm until needed.

Preheat the oven to 500°F.

Brush the bottom of the fish with the oil and place on a cookie sheet. Place in the oven and cook for approximately 9 to 11 minutes, or until the internal temperature is 120°F. If a crisp crust is desired, set the fish under the oven broiler for the final minute of cooking time. The salmon should have a crisp exterior and a tender interior. Remove from the oven and let cool slightly, 1 to 2 minutes.

Place the mashed potatoes in the center of 4 plates. Place the salmon on the potatoes.

Pour the hollandaise sauce over the salmon and then drizzle the lime cream over the sauce. Garnish with cilantro sprigs.

WINE:
The "life is too short" pick:
Dirler, Riesling, Spiegel, Grand Cru, Alsace, France 2009
The "just because it's inexpensive doesn't mean you're cheap" pick:
Chateau Ste. Michelle, Riesling, "Eroica," Columbia Valley, Washington 2009
Alternatives: *A rich and lively white that is off-dry (semi-sweet) to cut through the heat of the dish. French Chenin Blanc (Vouvray) or Oregon Pinot Gris.*

Cedar BBQ Plank Grilled Salmon
Serves 4

4 salmon pieces, 6 to 7 ounces, block cut, skin off
1 lemon quarter, cut into 2 wedges
2 tablespoons butter, melted
4 fresh Italian parsley sprigs
4 half-moon lemon slices, ½ inch thick

Salmon Dry Rub Seasoning
1 teaspoon lemon pepper
½ teaspoon granulated garlic
½ teaspoon dried whole tarragon leaves
½ teaspoon dried whole basil leaves
1½ teaspoons paprika
1½ teaspoons kosher salt
1 teaspoon packed light brown sugar

Special equipment: cedar BBQ grilling plank
        (page 25)

Prepare the Salmon Dry Rub Seasoning: Place all the ingredients in a spice grinder or mini food processor and process until well blended. Store in an airtight container at room temperature.

Between 2 and 12 hours before cooking the salmon, place it on waxed paper. Sprinkle both sides evenly with the dry rub (1½ teaspoons per piece). Press the seasonings into the salmon flesh. Refrigerate, uncovered, for at least 2 hours and up to 12 hours.

Soak the cedar plank in water for 1 to 2 hours, or until completely soaked through.

Preheat the grill to high.

Place the seasoned salmon on the soaked cedar plank, leaving space between the pieces. Squeeze the lemon wedges over the salmon.

Turn down the grill heat to medium-high. Place the plank on the grill and close the grill lid.

Cook for 8 to 12 minutes, depending on the thickness of the salmon, to an internal temperature of 120-125°F. Check the plank every 2 to 3 minutes to ensure that it has not caught fire. If it has, use a spray bottle of water to put the fire out, and continue cooking.

Remove the plank from the grill with tongs and place on a baking sheet. Be careful — the plank will have hot coals on the bottom. Brush the salmon with the melted butter, then garnish with the parsley sprigs and lemon slices.

Wine:
The "life is too short" pick:
Cayuse, Grenache, "God Only Knows," Walla Walla Valley, Washington 2007
The "just because it's inexpensive doesn't mean you're cheap" pick:
Borsao, Garnacha, "Tres Picos," Campo de Borja, Spain 2009
Alternatives: *A red wine with white-pepper-dusted black cherry notes and moderate tannin. Washington Grenache or Australian Grenache.*

WINE:
The "life is too short" pick:
Jermann, Pinot Grigio, Friuli, Italy 2009
The "just because it's inexpensive doesn't mean you're cheap" pick:
Franz Haas, Pinot Grigio, "Kris," Friuli, Italy 2009
Alternatives: *A crisp white with aromas and flavors of white flowers, red apples and almonds. Dry Oregon Pinot Gris or Spanish Albariño.*

SHRIMP WITH SPAGHETTI SQUASH
SERVES 4

1½- to 2-pound spaghetti squash,
        to yield 3 cups of strands
20 slices of zucchini, diagonally cut 3 inches
        long by ½ inch thick
6 tablespoons olive oil, divided
2 teaspoons sea salt, divided
1¾ teaspoons freshly ground black pepper,
        divided
½ cup unsalted butter
½ cup diced red bell peppers (¼-inch pieces)
20 white shrimp (21/25 count),
        shelled, deveined, loosely skewered tail
        to head on 2 skewers
½ cup Basil-Garlic Butter, softened (page 82)
4 fresh basil sprigs

PESTO BEURRE BLANC
⅜ cup Beurre Blanc (page 84 – make half of
        the recipe)
2 tablespoons Basil Pesto (page 29), at room
        temperature

Cut the squash in half and remove the seeds. Place upside down in a steamer pan and steam for 12 to 14 minutes, or until the spaghetti strands can be removed easily. Cool slightly and then pull out all of the spaghetti strands. Spread the strands on a sheet pan to cool. Do not use any chunks of squash. Set aside until needed.

Prepare the Pesto Beurre Blanc: Prepare the beurre blanc. Add the pesto to the warm beurre blanc. Keep warm until needed.

Preheat the grill or a grill pan to medium-high.

Brush the zucchini slices with 2 tablespoons olive oil and season with 1 teaspoon salt and ¾ teaspoon pepper. Place on the hot grill or grill pan and cook for 45 to 60 seconds, then change the angle to create diamond grill marks and cook for another 45 to 60 seconds. Turn the slices over and repeat the process. Don't overcook — keep the zucchini al dente, very al dente, if it is to be reheated (see note). Place 5 zucchini slices on each plate, in a star pattern.

Melt the butter and 4 tablespoons olive oil in a sauté pan over medium heat. Add the bell peppers and spaghetti squash, and cook until heated through but the spaghetti strands are still evident — not mushy! Season with ½ teaspoon salt. Evenly distribute and mound the squash in the center of each plate, slightly overlapping the zucchini.

Brush the skewered shrimp with softened basil-garlic butter and season with ¼ teaspoon salt and ½ teaspoon pepper. Place the shrimp on the grill. Cook on medium-high for 2 minutes, then turn them over and baste with basil-garlic butter. Cook to 120-125°F, then baste and season the shrimp with ¼ teaspoon salt and ½ teaspoon pepper before removing from the grill. Twist and spin the skewers to remove the shrimp.

Place the shrimp around the outside edges of the spaghetti squash, each shrimp propped up on a zucchini slice, with the tail side pointed up. Drizzle the shrimp and zucchini with the pesto beurre blanc. Garnish with the basil sprigs.

Note: Reheat the zucchini in the oven at 350°F.

SIZZLING DUNGENESS CRAB CAKES
SERVES 4

THAI SWEET-N-SOUR SAUCE
¾ teaspoon cornstarch
2 tablespoons water
¼ cup sugar
1 tablespoon plus 1½ teaspoons rice vinegar
2 tablespoons Mae Ploy Thai sweet chili sauce
¾ teaspoon Thai fish sauce
¾ teaspoon fresh lime juice
¼ teaspoon finely minced peeled fresh ginger
⅛ teaspoon finely minced fresh garlic

THAI BEURRE BLANC SAUCE
1½ teaspoons finely minced shallots
1 tablespoon white wine vinegar
½ cup Chablis or similar dry white wine
¼ cup whipping cream
6 tablespoons unsalted butter, cut into 2-inch chunks
¼ teaspoon sea or kosher salt
Thai Sweet-n-Sour Sauce, warmed

CRAB CAKES
¼ cup unsalted butter
3 tablespoons minced onion (1⁄16-inch pieces)
3 tablespoons minced celery (1⁄16-inch pieces)
3 tablespoons minced carrot (1⁄16-inch pieces)
6 tablespoons minced yellow, red and green bell pepper (1⁄16-inch pieces)
¼ cup whipping cream
1 pound Dungeness crab meat
1 egg yolk
¼ teaspoon ground black pepper
1 teaspoon sea salt
1½ cups flour
3 eggs
1 cup milk
4 cups panko (Japanese bread crumbs)
½ cup clarified butter (page 135)

For serving:
1 cup daikon or radish sprouts
4 ounces sliced pink pickled ginger, rolled into 4 roses

Prepare the Thai Sweet-n-Sour Sauce: Combine the cornstarch and water. Set aside. Combine all the other ingredients in a saucepan and cook over medium heat for 3 to 4 minutes. Add the well-mixed cornstarch and water blend to the pan and cook for 2 to 3 minutes, or until the sauce has a slightly thickened texture. Refrigerate until needed.

Prepare the Thai Beurre Blanc Sauce: Combine the shallots, vinegar and wine in a saucepan. Cook over medium heat until reduced to a light syrup consistency (approximately 90 percent).

Add the cream and cook until reduced by 60 percent over medium-high heat.

Reduce the heat to low. Add the butter cubes one at a time, whipping until melted. Strain the sauce through a fine-mesh strainer. Then add the salt and the warm Thai Sweet-n-Sour Sauce.

Prepare the Crab Cakes: Heat the butter in a sauté pan over medium heat (do not brown). Add the onion, celery, carrot and bell peppers. Sauté until tender. Add the cream and cook for 2 to 3 minutes, letting it reduce slightly. Transfer to a large mixing bowl and let cool for 5 minutes. Stir in the crab meat, egg yolk, pepper and salt. Chill for 30 to 45 minutes or up to 2 days. This can also be frozen for up to a month.

Place the flour in a shallow bowl. In another bowl, combine the eggs and milk, and beat until blended. Place the panko in another shallow bowl.

Divide the crab mixture into 24 equal portions and shape into balls. Start the breading process by first dusting each crab cake ball with flour. Quickly dip the crab cake into the egg wash and then place in the panko. Gently press and mold the crumbs into the cake, forming a ½-inch-thick round patty.

Note: We use a 2-inch-round, ¾-inch-tall mold to form and press the crab cakes. This is not required, but it will help your crab cakes maintain their shape.

To cook the crab cakes, working in batches, heat some of the clarified butter in a sauté pan over medium heat (don't allow it to smoke). Place the crab cakes in the heated pan, swirling them to create even browning, and cook for 1½ to 2 minutes, or until the edges are golden brown. Turn the cakes over, swirl again to create even browning, and cook for 1½ to 2 minutes. Remove from the pan and place on paper towels.

To serve, place some beurre blanc sauce on the front half of each plate. Arrange 6 crab cakes on the sauce. Garnish the plate with the daikon sprouts and pickled ginger behind the crab cakes.

WINE:
The "life is too short" pick:
DeLille Cellars, Chaleur Estate (Blanc), Columbia Valley, Washington 2010
The "just because it's inexpensive doesn't mean you're cheap" pick:
Chateau Ste. Michelle, Sauvignon Blanc, Columbia Valley, Washington 2009
Alternatives: *A fresh and lively white that has some sweet fruit notes to balance a bit of heat from the spicy element of the dish. New Zealand Sauvignon Blanc or French Sauvignon/Semillon blend (white Bordeaux).*

KING CRAB AU GRATIN
SERVES 4

CRISPY AU GRATIN TOPPING MIX
¼ cup shredded Tillamook medium Cheddar cheese
¼ cup shredded Asiago cheese
¼ cup finely crushed or grated garlic croutons (page 81)

ONION CREAM SAUCE
½ cup salted butter
½ cup very finely minced sweet white onion
3 cups heavy whipping cream (36% butter fat)
¼ teaspoon kosher salt
⅛ teaspoon ground white pepper

ROASTED GARLIC PUREE
3 tablespoons plus 2 teaspoons roasted garlic (page 23), hard stem ends removed
1 teaspoon olive oil

ROASTED GARLIC MASHED POTATOES
1½ pounds Yukon Gold potatoes, peeled and quartered
4 tablespoons salted butter
½ cup half-and-half
¾ teaspoon kosher salt
¼ teaspoon ground white pepper

CRAB MIXTURE
¼ cup minced onions (⅛-inch pieces)
¼ cup minced celery (⅛-inch pieces)
3 cups Alaskan king crab meat – a mixture of leg, knuckle and claw meat
¾ cup shredded Fontina cheese
4 fresh Italian parsley sprigs

Prepare the Crispy au Gratin Topping Mix: Combine all the ingredients and mix until blended. Refrigerate until needed.

Prepare the Onion Cream Sauce: Melt the butter over low heat in a heavy-gauge saucepan. Add the onion and simmer for 5 to 8 minutes, or until the onion softens. Don't let it brown at all.

Add the cream. Bring to a simmer, then continue to simmer for 30 minutes, letting the cream reduce slowly by about 20 percent. Stir the sauce often to avoid scorching. Remove from the heat and add the salt and pepper. Refrigerate, stirring often to ensure that the butter does not separate from the sauce. Keep in the refrigerator until needed.

Prepare the Roasted Garlic Puree: Place all the ingredients in a mini food processor and puree. Refrigerate, covered, until needed.

Prepare the Roasted Garlic Mashed Potatoes: Boil the potatoes until tender, approximately 15 to 20 minutes. Drain well.

In a heavy-gauge saucepan, combine the butter and half-and-half. Warm over medium heat until the butter is melted, being careful not to brown. Keep warm until needed.

Place the potatoes in a countertop mixer. Use the paddle attachment to break up the potatoes. Then switch to the whip attachment and whip on medium-high speed, gradually adding the butter-cream liquid.

Add the seasonings and the roasted garlic puree. Whip the potatoes on medium speed until mashed and creamy. Keep warm until needed.

Prepare the Crab Mixture: Place the Onion Cream Sauce, onions and celery in a sauté pan. Bring to a boil over medium-high heat, then reduce the heat and cook at a low simmer until the sauce is reduced by about 25 percent, approximately 2 to 3 minutes. Add the crab and toss until well coated. Add the Fontina and mix into the sauce until fully incorporated. The sauce should be thick and creamy, completely coating the crab, but not over-reduced. If over-reduced, the sauce will start to break. If this happens, add a little cream — this will help, as the sauce will continue to reduce in the bowl.

To assemble the dish, preheat the broiler.

Evenly layer the bottom of 4 heat-resistant pasta bowls or baking dishes with the potatoes. Place under the broiler until the top is lightly browned.

Place the sauce-coated crab on top of the potatoes, mounding the crab in the center and leaving some potatoes showing around the edges. Top the crab with the crispy au gratin topping.

Place in the oven under the broiler, close to the element, for 60 to 90 seconds, or until lightly browned and crisp but not burned. Place the very hot pasta bowls on plates. Garnish with the parsley sprigs on top.

WINE:
The "life is too short" pick:
François Raveneau, "Les Clos," Chablis, France 2002
The "just because it's inexpensive doesn't mean you're cheap" pick:
Lafon, Mâcon-Villages, Burgundy (Chardonnay), France 2009
Alternatives: *A rich white wine with high acidity and no oak. Unoaked California Chardonnay or rich Italian Pinot Grigio.*

Yes, I introduced him to sushi experience — first day he cut his finger! At Triples we had a small space, a little island for two people. Well, John is not petite. Working with him was remarkable — he really knows how to move.

I have traveled with him a bit, and I got to know him personally, another side of him. He is a family guy and always does good deeds for people, always helping people.

I like working with John — his sincerity. He is an up-front guy: up-front good and up-front bad, a no-nonsense manager. If you are good, he will tell you, if bad, he will tell you. Working with him is quite rewarding. He is a very fair person. Sometimes he yells — you can either confront him or hide.

DAVID PUTAPORTIWON
RAW BAR CHEF / PARTNER
SEASTAR RESTAURANT & RAW BAR

I have known John for 23 years. I started with John at Triples as a dishwasher. The next year he opened Palisade and I stayed at Triples. He then called and asked if I wanted to work with him at Palisade as a pantry cook and I said OK. I left Palisade for a year and a half, and had another job. In 1997, I went back to Palisade and asked him if he had any job openings. It was September. John said, "Oh, you know this is a bad time of year for restaurants." I left the restaurant and a couple of hours later he called and asked if I could start tomorrow — I said OK.

He is a really nice guy. He is always helping people. When you go to him, he is always thinking how can I help. He has an open mind, your ideas he will listen to; he accepts everybody and everybody's ideas. I have learned a lot from him. I am lucky to work with him. I will work for him until I retire.

LEE LOI WONG
SOUS-CHEF / PARTNER
SEASTAR RESTAURANT & RAW BAR

PASTA & RISOTTO

Capellini with Mussels, Shrimp and Saffron Cream
Serves 4

½ pound capellini
Olive oil
3 cups Fish Stock (page 119), reduced to 1½ cups
24 fresh mussels, scrubbed and debearded
24 white Gulf shrimp (21/25 count), peeled, deveined, tail on
1 cup cooked baby artichoke hearts cut into eighths, fresh blanched or canned (see note)
2 teaspoons sea salt
1½ teaspoons freshly ground black pepper
¼ cup Red Pepper Rouille
20 fresh Italian parsley leaves

Red Pepper Rouille
2 teaspoons fresh white bread crumbs (¼-inch pieces, crust removed)
1 egg yolk
3 tablespoons peeled, chopped roasted red bell pepper (page 23)
1 teaspoon minced fresh garlic
⅛ teaspoon cayenne pepper
¼ teaspoon sea salt
¼ teaspoon ground black pepper
2 teaspoons fresh lemon juice
2 tablespoons olive oil

Note: To blanch artichokes, trim the artichokes, then cook in boiling water to cover for 2 to 3 minutes, or until tender.

Saffron Cream Sauce
3 cups Fish Stock (page 119)
⅜ teaspoon minced saffron
1 cup heavy cream
1 tablespoon unsalted butter
1 tablespoon flour
¼ teaspoon sea salt
⅛ teaspoon ground white pepper

Prepare the Red Pepper Rouille: Place the bread in a food processor and process to ¹⁄₁₆-inch pieces. Add the egg yolk, roasted pepper, garlic, cayenne pepper, salt and black pepper. Process the mixture for 30 seconds.

With the processor running, gradually add the lemon juice and then the olive oil. The mixture will slowly emulsify and thicken. Transfer to a squeeze bottle and refrigerate until needed.

Note: Rouille should be made at least 4 hours in advance, which allows the sauce to thicken and the flavors to blend. It will keep in the refrigerator for 2 to 3 days. Leftover rouille is good with chicken and shrimp, or spread on a sandwich.

Prepare the Saffron Cream Sauce: Place the fish stock in a heavy-gauge saucepan. Add the saffron. Bring to a simmer, then cook until reduced by 50 percent, approximately 15 minutes. Add the cream and bring to a simmer.

In another heavy-gauge saucepan, melt the butter over medium heat. Add the flour and cook for 1 minute. Do not brown the roux. Slowly add the cream mixture to the roux, stirring constantly. Bring to a simmer until it thickens slightly. Add the salt and white pepper. Remove from the heat. Let cool, then refrigerate until needed.

Bring a large pot of water to a boil. Place the capellini in the water and cook for 1 minute. Strain the capellini — but don't rinse — then spread out on a cookie sheet and drizzle with a little olive oil so it won't stick together or continue to cook.

Place the reduced fish stock and saffron cream sauce in a large sauté pan over medium-high heat. Heat for 30 seconds, then add the mussels and bring to a boil. Reduce the heat, cover, and cook for 1 minute, or until the mussels begin to open.

Add the shrimp and cook for 30 seconds. Add the artichoke hearts, pasta, salt and pepper. Toss until well coated and heated through. Remove from the heat.

Evenly distribute the pasta in the center of 4 bowls and pull some of the mussels and shrimp up on top of the pasta. If necessary, reduce the remaining sauce slightly, then pour over the top of everything. Drizzle the rouille over the pasta and seafood. Place the parsley leaves on top.

PICKING YOUR SHELLFISH:

Remember that any fresh seafood, from fish to shellfish, should always smell like a fresh sea breeze, not strong and fishy. From oysters to clams to mussels, they should always be closed, or close quickly when tapped on the shell.

KEEPING SHELLFISH FRESH:

Always store shellfish refrigerated, but not frozen. Store with a moist clean cloth covering the shellfish, in a perforated pan with a bottom pan to collect any juices. Clams and mussels can be held for up to 24 hours before use.

Oysters should always be kept "cup down," which means that the cupped side of the oyster shell should always be the bottom shell. This way the natural juices stay in the oyster. They can be held this way for up to three days. If the oysters are not held cup down, the juices will leak out and they will dry out quickly.

Again, fish should have a fresh sea-breeze smell, not fishy or strong. The flesh should be bright in color, not graying, and feel clean to the touch, not sticky or mealy.

WINE:
The "life is too short" pick:
Schiopetto, Pinot Grigio, "Collio," Friuli, Italy 2008
The "just because it's inexpensive doesn't mean you're cheap" pick:
Lemelson, Pinot Gris, "Tikka's Run," Willamette Valley, Oregon 2009
Alternatives: *A white wine with zesty acidity and rich fruit flavors of apples and pears. Spanish Albariño or Austrian Grüner Veltliner.*

Mini Penne Pasta with Heirloom Tomatoes, Basil, Artichoke and Shrimp

SERVES 4

½ cup extra-virgin olive oil

2 tablespoons thinly shaved whole garlic slices

2 cups diced heirloom tomatoes, assorted colors (½-inch pieces)

1 pound mini penne rigate, cooked al dente

1 cup quartered cooked artichoke hearts

1½ cups white shrimp pieces (½ to ¾ inch)

¼ cup Vegetable Stock (page 118)

1½ teaspoons sea salt

1 teaspoon coarsely ground black pepper

½ cup thinly sliced fresh basil

4 tablespoons freshly grated Parmigiano-Reggiano cheese

4 fresh basil sprigs

Heat the olive oil in a sauté pan over medium heat. Add the garlic and cook for 15 seconds. Do not brown!

Add the tomatoes and cook for 1 minute. Then add the cooked penne and cook for 1 minute, tossing lightly a couple of times. Add the artichoke hearts, shrimp, vegetable stock, salt and pepper. Cook until the shrimp is tender and firm.

Add the basil and toss lightly. Place in pasta bowls. Top with Parmigiano-Reggiano. Garnish with basil sprigs.

WINE:
The "life is too short" pick:
Jermann, "Vintage Tunina," Friuli, Italy 2008
The "just because it's inexpensive doesn't mean you're cheap" pick:
Terlano, Pinot Grigio, Alto Adige, Italy 2009
Alternatives: *A white wine with vibrant acidity and flavors and aromas of apples and baked almonds. Oregon Pinot Gris or Spanish Albariño.*

LINGUINE WITH TOMATOES, BASIL AND ARTICHOKES
SERVES 4

½ cup extra-virgin olive oil
¼ cup very thinly shaved whole garlic slices
2 cups diced Roma tomatoes (½-inch pieces)
2 cups diced heirloom tomatoes (½-inch pieces)
4 cups cooked linguine (al dente)
1½ cups quartered cooked artichoke hearts
¼ cup Vegetable Stock (page 118)
1½ teaspoons sea salt
1 teaspoon coarsely ground black pepper
½ cup packed thinly sliced basil
¼ cup grated Parmigiano-Reggiano cheese
4 fresh basil sprigs

Place the olive oil in a large sauté pan over medium heat. Add the garlic and cook for 15 seconds. Do not brown!

Add the tomatoes and cook for 1 minute. Then add the linguine and cook for 1 minute, tossing lightly a couple of times. Add the artichoke hearts, vegetable stock, salt and pepper. Cook until well coated.

Add the basil, toss lightly, and place in 4 pasta bowls, using tongs to bring some of the artichokes and tomatoes to the top of the pasta. Top with grated cheese. Garnish with basil sprigs.

Note: This is a great lacto-ovo-vegetarian pasta. Without the cheese, it is also a great vegan preparation. As I always state, my recipes are a base — if there's something you want to add or something you want to take away, then you should do that. This is a good example of a recipe that can be changed and adapted to suit your taste. Add chicken or shrimp, olives or pine nuts — all would be excellent additions to this pasta.

WINE:
The "life is too short" pick:
Jermann, "Vintage Tunina," Friuli, Italy 2008
The "just because it's inexpensive doesn't mean you're cheap" pick:
Terlano, Pinot Grigio, Alto Adige, Italy 2009
Alternatives: *A white wine with vibrant acidity and flavors and aromas of apples and baked almonds. Oregon Pinot Gris or Spanish Albariño.*

DUNGENESS CRAB AND SWEET CORN RISOTTO
SERVES 4

2 tablespoons olive oil

2 tablespoons minced shallots

3 tablespoons minced leeks, white and light green parts only

1 pound Arborio rice

1 cup Chablis or other dry white wine

1½ cups fresh corn kernels, shocked in boiling water for 30 seconds, cooled, and
refrigerated until needed

¾ cup whipping cream

2 teaspoons chopped fresh thyme leaves

1 pound Dungeness crab meat – mixed claw, leg and body meat

¼ cup sliced chives (⅛-inch pieces)

1 teaspoon sea salt

½ teaspoon freshly ground black pepper

4 fresh thyme sprigs

12 chive spears (4-inch-long diagonal slices)

BASIL OIL

3 tablespoons extra-virgin olive oil

¼ cup thinly sliced fresh basil leaves

CORN STOCK

7 cups Vegetable Stock (page 118)

2 ears of corn, broken into 2-inch pieces

½ cup fresh corn kernels

¼ cup diced carrots (½-inch pieces)

¼ cup diced celery (½-inch pieces)

¼ cup diced onion (½-inch pieces)

1½ teaspoons chopped fresh thyme leaves

¾ teaspoon sea or kosher salt

Special equipment: fine-mesh strainer; cheesecloth

Prepare the Basil Oil: Combine the oil and basil. Let sit at room temperature for 24 hours. Place in a blender and puree. Strain through a fine-mesh strainer lined with cheesecloth. Store at room temperature.

Prepare the Corn Stock: Place all the ingredients in a large stockpot and bring to a boil. Reduce the heat, cover, and let simmer for 20 minutes. Remove from the heat, take out the cob pieces, and puree the remaining stock in a blender. Strain through a fine-mesh strainer. Let cool, then refrigerate until needed.

To prepare the risotto, heat the olive oil in a large heavy-gauge sauté pan over medium-high heat. Add the shallots and leeks, and cook, stirring, for 30 seconds — don't brown. Add the rice and sauté, stirring, until it is well coated, approximately 1 to 2 minutes. Add the wine and cook until the liquid is almost gone.

Add 1 cup of corn stock, then lower the heat and simmer, working the ingredients with a rubber spatula, until the liquid is almost gone, about 2 to 3 minutes. Continue adding the stock 1 cup at a time and following this procedure until the rice is al dente and has a creamy medium-thick consistency.

When making risotto, sometimes you need less stock and sometimes more. This will be based on how quickly you evaporate the liquid in the pan. Add or delete stock as necessary to ensure that the rice is creamy but still al dente before continuing to the next step.

Add the corn and cook for 1 minute, until it is warmed through. Add the cream and fresh thyme, and cook for 1 to 2 minutes. Add the crab and cook for 1 minute, just until thickened slightly, then add the sliced chives, salt and pepper.

Serve in pasta bowls. Drizzle with the basil oil and garnish with the thyme sprigs and chive spears in the center.

WINE:
The "life is too short" pick:
Franck Peillot, "Altesse," Bugey, France 2009
The "just because it's inexpensive doesn't mean you're cheap" pick:
Pierre Boniface, "Apremont," Savoie, France 2009
Alternatives: *A white wine that balances rich red apple and earth notes with zippy acidity to match the delicate crab and earthy corn components of the dish. Spanish Albariño or dry Oregon Pinot Gris.*

LOBSTER MACARONI AND CHEESE
SERVES 4

2 Maine lobsters, 1½ to 1¾ pounds each
3 cups cooked large elbow macaroni (al dente)
¾ cup shredded creamy-style Fontina cheese
1 tablespoon plus 1 teaspoon fresh tarragon leaves (25 to 35 leaves)
6 ounces Délice de Bourgogne cheese, cut into 4 even slices
4 fresh chervil sprigs

ONION CREAM SAUCE
8 tablespoons salted butter
½ cup very finely minced sweet white onion
1 quart heavy whipping cream (36% butterfat)
½ teaspoon kosher salt
⅛ teaspoon ground white pepper

Délice de Bourgogne is an award-winning triple-cream cow's milk cheese from France. Luckily, it's carried at Costco. This cheese is very creamy. If it's difficult to slice, you can freeze it for 30 minutes before slicing.

CRISPY CHEESE TOPPING
5 tablespoons shredded medium Cheddar cheese
5 tablespoons shredded Asiago cheese
6 tablespoons finely ground or grated Garlic Croutons (page 81)

Blanch the lobsters for 4 to 5 minutes in boiling water to cover. Remove the meat and cut into 1-inch pieces. Squeeze the legs with a rolling pin to push out the meat. Refrigerate until needed.

Prepare the Onion Cream Sauce: Using a heavy-gauge saucepan, melt the butter over low heat. Add the minced onion and simmer for 5 to 8 minutes, until the onion softens. It's important that it doesn't brown at all.

Add the cream and simmer for 45 minutes, letting the cream reduce slowly by about 25 percent. Stir the sauce often to avoid scorching. Remove from the heat and add the salt and pepper. Transfer the sauce to an ice bath, stirring often as it cools to incorporate the butter into the sauce and prevent separation. Refrigerate until needed.

Prepare the Crispy Cheese Topping: Mix all the ingredients together and refrigerate until needed.

To assemble the macaroni and cheese, place the sauce in a large sauté pan over medium-high heat and bring to a boil. Add the cooked pasta and bring to a boil, then reduce the heat to medium and cook to reduce the sauce slightly, about 10 percent. Add the Fontina and mix into the sauce until completely incorporated. The sauce should be thick and creamy, completely coating the pasta. Stir in the lobster and tarragon, and let it heat for 1 minute. Make sure the sauce isn't over-reduced! If this happens, add a little cream, as it will continue to reduce in the bowl.

Preheat the oven broiler. Place the pasta in a large heat-resistant pasta bowl and add the topping.

Place under the broiler, close to the heat. Cook until the topping is crisp and lightly browned, being careful not to burn it. Remove and immediately garnish the top with the slices of Délice de Bourgogne and chervil sprigs.

Chervil is the preferred garnish, but if it's not available, leftover tarragon or even Italian parsley would make a nice substitute.

Maine lobster should be purchased live and should be cooked while it is still alive. Frozen lobster meat or frozen lobster tail can be substituted, but fresh live Maine is preferable. You will need 1 pound of meat. If you are using raw frozen meat, it must be thawed and blanched before using. If you are using frozen cooked lobster, thaw it first.

WINE:
The "life is too short" pick:
Dauvissat-Camus, Chablis, "Les Clos," Burgundy, France 2007
The "just because it's inexpensive doesn't mean you're cheap" pick:
Verget, Mâcon-Villages, Burgundy, France 2009
Alternatives: *A white wine that has enough racy acidity to balance the richness of the dish and enough fruit to balance the delicacy of the lobster. Unoaked Chardonnay.*

GRILLING

THERE ARE MANY different ways to grill. Some people call cooking foods on a flat-top grill grilling, but that is not what I'm referring to when I speak of grilling. As stated in many of the recipes, we want you to grill on a hot grill pan, or a gas barbecue, or a live-flame barbecue. I prefer the live-flame barbecue, but have also used a grilling pan and the gas barbecue.

If you're using a grilling pan, one with a grated surface, preheat the pan over medium-high heat. This will ensure that you are able to get nice caramelized grill marks on the foods you are cooking, and seal in the juices. When using the grill pan for items that are thicker than ¾ inch, it is best to first get your good grill marks, and then finish the cooking process in a 400°F oven.

Gas grills should be preheated over medium-high or even high heat, until the grates are very hot. Again, this will help seal the foods and produce nice grill marks. Lower the heat to medium halfway through the cooking; this will prevent charring of the foods before they are finished cooking. Cooking with the lid closed will help finish the cooking process, similar to using an oven.

Charcoal grills are similar to gas grills in that you want to get a very hot fire and start cooking just as the coals are at the peak of their intensity. This will seal in the juices. Then as the coals naturally cool, so will the cooking surface, and you can avoid overcharring your foods. Covering the grill will produce an ovenlike finish, but you have to be careful with live fire, as it needs oxygen to keep cooking.

MEAT & POULTRY

BEEF TENDERLOIN WITH WASABI TERIYAKI
SERVES 4

8 beef tenderloin medallions, 3 ounces each,
  ¾ to 1 inch thick (1½ pounds total)
1½ cups Teriyaki Marinade (page 86)
10 snow peas, stemmed and sliced diagonally
  in half
20 paper-thin slices fresh pineapple – peel
  the pineapple, cut in half lengthwise,
  remove the core, and slice
4 cups cooked sticky white rice
½ cup Wasabi-Teriyaki Glaze, warmed
1 teaspoon *each* black and toasted white
  sesame seeds, mixed
¼ cup diagonally sliced green onions
  (1 to 2 inches long by ⅛ inch thick)

WASABI-TERIYAKI GLAZE
MAKES 1¼ CUPS
1 cup Terikayi Marinade (page 86)
1 tablespoon cornstarch
1 tablespoon wasabi powder
2 tablespoons water
¼ cup pineapple juice

Special equipment: 1-cup Pyrex glass baking
  dish (optional)

Place the tenderloin pieces in the marinade and marinate, refrigerated, for 2 hours. Then remove the meat from the marinade, place in a drain pan or colander, and let drain for 10 minutes. Refrigerate until needed, up to 24 hours.

Prepare the Wasabi-Teriyaki Glaze: Strain the teriyaki marinade and place in a saucepan.

Blend together the cornstarch, wasabi, water and pineapple juice. Gradually stir into the marinade. Heat over medium-high heat, stirring frequently, until the sauce thickens.

Keep warm until needed, or chill and then reheat. Add more water to thin the sauce if necessary. This will keep for up to 4 weeks, covered, in the refrigerator.

Preheat the grill or a grill pan to medium-high.

Place the beef medallions on the hot grill or grill pan and cook, turning to create diamond marks, on both sides until cooked to taste, approximately 2½ to 3 minutes on each side for medium-rare.

Place the snow peas in boiling water and cook for 1 minute. Drain.

On 4 plates, place the pineapple slices and snow peas around the outer edges, alternating pineapple slices and snow peas.

Pack 1 cup of warm rice into the glass dish and unmold in the center of each plate, barely overlapping the inside edges of the pineapple and snow peas.

Drizzle the rice, pineapple and snow peas with 6 tablespoons (⅜ cup) of the warm glaze.

Then place the beef medallions on top of the rice and drizzle with 2 tablepoons of the glaze. Sprinkle the sesame seeds over everything, and garnish the meat with the green onions.

WINE:
  The "life is too short" pick:
  Müller-Catoir, Riesling, Spätlese, Pfalz, Germany 2007
  The "just because it's inexpensive doesn't mean you're cheap" pick:
  St. Urbans-Hof, Riesling, QbA, Mosel, Germany 2009
  Alternatives: *Yep, a white wine with beef! Remember, we are pairing the wine to the most prominent flavors on the plate — in this instance, the wasabi and the teriyaki.*

TOP SIRLOIN WITH POTATO PUREE
SERVES 4

¼ cup Veal Demi-Glace (page 86)
4 top sirloin steaks, 8 to 9 ounces each, 1 to 1½ inches thick (preferably USDA Prime)
2 tablespoons Steak Seasoning Blend
20 diagonally sliced chive pieces (¾ inch long)

ROASTED CIPOLLINI ONIONS
8 cipollini onions, peeled, tops and bottoms slightly trimmed
4 teaspoons olive oil

ROASTED CREMINI MUSHROOMS
4 large (2-inch) cremini mushrooms, stems cut off at the base
1 tablespoon clarified butter (page 135)
1 teaspoon Seafood Seasoning Blend (page 139)

Prepare the Roasted Cipollini Onions:
Preheat the oven to 400°F.

Coat the onions with olive oil. Place on a sheet pan, core side down, in the oven. Roast until lightly browned on top and softened, approximately 25 to 30 minutes. Keep warm until needed.

Prepare the Roasted Cremini Mushrooms:
Preheat the oven to 400°F.

Toss the mushroom caps in the clarified butter. Lay them stem side down on a sheet pan and sprinkle evenly with the seasoning blend. Roast for 9 to 12 minutes, or until tender. Remove from the oven and keep warm until needed.

To prepare the steaks, preheat an outdoor grill or an indoor grill pan to medium-high.

Preheat the oven to 400°F.

Place the demi-glace in a saucepan over low heat and cook until reduced by half. Set aside.

Season each steak with 1½ teaspoons of the steak seasoning. Place the steaks on the hot grill or in the grill pan and cook until marks form (about 2 to 3 minutes), then change the angle of the steaks to create diamond marks and cook for another 2 to 3 minutes. Turn the steaks over and cook for 2 to 3 minutes, then change the angle and cook for another 2 to 3 minutes, or until cooked to taste. Remove from the grill and let rest.

Place the roasted onions and mushrooms in the preheated oven and reheat, approximately 3 to 4 minutes.

Place equal amounts of the potato puree in the bottom of 4 bowls. Next place the steaks directly in the center. Drizzle 1½ teaspoons of the reduced veal demi-glace across each steak and onto the potato puree as well. Place 2 onions on each steak, then top with a mushroom. Garnish with the chives.

POTATO PUREE
SERVES 4

12 tablespoons unsalted butter
6 tablespoons half-and-half
¼ cup Chicken Stock (page 120)
2 teaspoons kosher salt
18 ounces russet potatoes
½ cup Butter Sauce (page 82)

In a heavy-gauge saucepan, melt the butter
over medium heat. Add the half-and-half,
chicken stock and salt. Cook until heated,
being careful not to brown. Keep warm until
needed.

Wash the potatoes, then peel completely clean,
leaving no skin. Cut into 2-inch pieces.

Cook the potatoes in boiling water to cover
until tender, approximately 15 minutes. Drain,
place on a sheet pan, and let cool slightly.

Pour half of the liquid into a blender (a Vitamix
is the best option). Add half of the potatoes.
Puree for 30 to 45 seconds. Remove from the
blender and push through a fine double-mesh
strainer. Repeat with the remaining potatoes.

Stir the butter sauce into the pureed potatoes.
Keep warm until needed.

STEAK SEASONING BLEND
MAKES 2¼ CUPS

1½ cups Diamond kosher salt
¼ cup coarsely ground black pepper
¼ cup granulated onion
¼ cup granulated garlic

Combine and blend all the ingredients.

Store in an airtight container at room
temperature for up to 6 months. If the
mixture cakes, that's okay — just break
it up with your fingers.

WINE:
The "life is too short" pick:
Quilceda Creek, Cabernet Sauvignon, Columbia Valley, Washington 2005
The "just because it's inexpensive doesn't mean you're cheap" pick:
Columbia Crest, Cabernet Sauvignon, "Grand Estates," Columbia Valley, Washington 2008
Alternatives: *A red with polished tannin to balance the richness of the sirloin and opulence of the
potatoes. French Cabernet Sauvignon (Bordeaux) or California Cabernet Sauvignon.*

SOUTH AMERICAN PEPPER STEAK

SERVES 4

4 top sirloin strip steaks, 6 ounces each, 1 to 1½ inches thick, 2 by 4 inches

4 teaspoons Steak Seasoning Blend (page 177), divided

¼ cup canola oil

1 cup sliced sweet onion (¼-inch strips sliced with the grain)

½ cup red bell pepper strips (¼ inch)

½ cup green bell pepper strips (¼ inch)

¼ cup roasted garlic cloves, cut in half (page 23)

¼ cup Tomatillo-Chipotle Sauce

¾ cup Veal Stock (page 121)

3 cups Red Chili Rice, warm (page 87)

6 tablespoons Chimichurri Salsa

4 large fresh cilantro sprigs

SOUTH AMERICAN STEAK MARINADE

2 small bay leaves

1 teaspoon ground cumin

1 teaspoon whole dried oregano

1 teaspoon whole dried thyme

½ teaspoon minced pan-toasted and reconstituted dried chipotle peppers (see note),
or pureed chipotles in adobo sauce

1½ teaspoons kosher salt

2 tablespoons coarsely chopped white onion

4 teaspoons minced fresh garlic

½ cup white wine vinegar

¼ cup canola oil

TOMATILLO-CHIPOTLE SAUCE

MAKES ½ CUP

½ cup tomatillos, husked

1 tablespoon minced pan-toasted and reconstituted dried chipotle peppers (see note),
or chipotles in adobo sauce

1½ teaspoons roasted garlic cloves (page 23)

¼ teaspoon kosher or sea salt

½ teaspoon ground cumin

¼ teaspoon coarsely ground black pepper

¼ teaspoon sugar

WINE:
The "life is too short" pick:
Turley, Zinfandel, Pesenti Vineyard, Paso Robles, California 2007
The "just because it's inexpensive doesn't mean you're cheap" pick:
Seghesio, Zinfandel, Sonoma, California 2009
Alternatives: *A red with big, jammy, spicy fruit and moderate tannin. Nero d'Avola from Italy or Malbec from Argentina.*

CHIMICHURRI SALSA

MAKES ½ CUP

2 teaspoons finely minced fresh garlic

2 small bay leaves, crushed very fine

1½ teaspoons finely minced (⅛ inch) jalapeño with seeds

6 tablespoons minced fresh Italian parsley (no stems)

3 tablespoons coarsely chopped fresh oregano (no stems)

⅜ teaspoon kosher salt

2 tablespoons white wine vinegar, divided

3 tablespoons olive oil

Prepare the South American Steak Marinade: Place all the ingredients except the oil in a blender. Process until pureed. Transfer to a bowl and whisk in the oil. Refrigerate, covered, until needed.

Place the steaks in a 2-inch-deep nonreactive pan. Cover the steaks with the marinade. Let marinate, covered, in the refrigerator for 12 hours or overnight, turning once to ensure even marination.

Prepare the Tomatillo-Chipotle Sauce: Preheat the oven broiler. Place the whole tomatillos in a roasting pan. Set under the broiler and roast to blacken on one side, approximately 5 minutes. Turn over and roast on the other side. Remove and let cool to room temperature. Combine chipotles, tomatillos, roasted garlic, salt, cumin, black pepper and sugar in a food processer and blend into a fine-textured puree. Refrigerate until needed.

Prepare the Chimichurri Salsa: Place the garlic, crushed bay leaves, jalapeños, parsley, oregano, salt and half the vinegar in a food processor. Process to a paste. Transfer to a mixing bowl and whisk in the remaining vinegar and the olive oil. Refrigerate, covered, until needed.

Remove the steaks from the marinade and transfer to a clean pan. Cover and refrigerate until needed.

Preheat the grill or a grill pan to medium-high.

Grill the marinated steaks for approximately 5 to 8 minutes per side for medium-rare, or to taste. Season the steaks with three-quarters of the steak seasoning during the grilling process. Turn the steaks to create diamond marks if possible.

Meanwhile, heat the oil in a sauté pan over medium-high heat. Add the onions and peppers, and sauté until the onions begin to brown. Add the roasted garlic cloves, tomatillo-chipotle sauce, veal stock and the remaining steak seasoning. Cook until reduced by 50 percent, to a medium sauce consistency.

To serve, place the rice on the upper left side of each plate. Pour the pepper-onion sauce over half of the plate, around the rice. Place a steak on top of the sauce, leaning on the rice. Dollop the chimichurri on the steak. Garnish with cilantro sprigs.

Note: Toast dried chipotles in a dry sauté pan or heavy skillet over medium heat, turning regularly and pressing flat with a spatula, for 30 to 45 seconds, or until the smell is evident. Transfer to a bowl, cover with hot water, and let soak for 30 minutes, stirring frequently to ensure even soaking. Drain and discard the water. Remove the stems from the chiles.

PLANK-ROASTED PORK LOIN CHOPS WITH ROASTED GARLIC AND ROSEMARY
SERVES 4

¼ cup whole garlic cloves, peeled
6 tablespoons olive oil, divided
4 boneless pork loin chops, 1½ inches thick (see note)
2 teaspoons salt, divided
1 teaspoon freshly ground black pepper, divided
2 tablespoons chopped fresh rosemary, divided
12 very small new red potatoes, quartered
¼ cup grated Parmesan cheese
4 fresh rosemary sprigs

Special equipment: 2 large cedar baking planks (page 25)

The first time I cooked pork chops on a cedar plank, I knew I would never have them any other way!

Preheat the oven to 375°F.

Toss the garlic cloves in 1 tablespoon olive oil. Place on a cedar plank and set in the oven for 12 to 15 minutes, or until golden brown. Remove from the oven and let cool. Then place in a food processor and add 2 tablespoons olive oil. Process until pureed.

Season the chops with half of the salt and pepper. Rub the roasted garlic puree all over the chops. Then sprinkle each chop with 1 teaspoon chopped rosemary. Place the chops on one of the planks.

Toss the potatoes with the remaining olive oil, salt, pepper and rosemary, and the Parmesan cheese. Place them on the other plank in a single layer.

Place both planks in the oven and bake for 18 to 20 minutes. Turn the chops over and return to the oven for 20 to 25 minutes, or until the internal temperature of the chops is 140°F and the potatoes are tender.

Transfer the potatoes and pork chops to individual plates. Garnish with the rosemary sprigs.

Note: Bone-in pork chops can also be used; they may take longer to cook.

WINE:
The "life is too short" pick:
Evening Land, Pinot Noir, "The Red Queen," Willamette Valley, Oregon 2008
The "just because it's inexpensive doesn't mean you're cheap" pick:
Lemelson, Pinot Noir, "Three Vineyards," Willamette Valley, Oregon 2008
Alternatives: *A red wine with vibrant red fruits, moderate tannin and creamy-toasty notes.*
Gamay (Beaujolais) from France or Garnacha from Spain.

PLANK-ROASTED PORK RIBS WITH CILANTRO CORN
SERVES 4

2 pounds baby back pork ribs, cut into 4 pieces
2 tablespoons BBQ Spice Rub (see note)
4 ears fresh corn on the cob, blanched and cut into sixteen 2-inch chunks
1 cup BBQ Sauce

BBQ SPICE RUB
MAKES ⅓ CUP
1¼ teaspoons ground allspice
1½ teaspoons ground star anise
1 teaspoon ground ginger
¾ teaspoon ground celery seed
2 teaspoons granulated onion
1 tablespoon granulated garlic
1 tablespoon ground paprika
1 tablespoon packed light brown sugar

BBQ SAUCE
MAKES 2 CUPS
2 tablespoons clarified butter (page 135)
½ cup diced onion (¼-inch pieces)
2 tablespoons ancho chili powder
½ teaspoon chipotle chili powder
1 tablespoon mild chili powder blend
3 tablespoons balsamic vinegar
2 tablespoons Dijon mustard
3 tablespoons packed light brown sugar
5 tablespoons molasses
1 teaspoon Worcestershire sauce
½ teaspoon minced fresh garlic
1 cup tomato puree
2 tablespoons honey

CILANTRO BUTTER
¼ pound unsalted butter, softened
½ teaspoon ground coriander
½ teaspoon mild chili powder
1 tablespoon minced fresh cilantro
½ teaspoon kosher salt (¼ teaspoon if using salted butter)

Special equipment: 2 large cedar baking planks (page 25)

Prepare the BBQ Spice Rub: Blend all ingredients together in a mini food processor or spice grinder until completely combined. Store for up to 2 months in an airtight container at room temperature.

Season each section of the ribs with 1½ teaspoons of the spice rub. Place in a pan where the air can circulate, uncovered or loosely covered, and refrigerate for 24 hours.

Prepare the BBQ Sauce: Heat the clarified butter in a saucepan over medium-high heat. Add the onion and chili powders, and sauté until the onion is soft and translucent. Add the vinegar, stirring to deglaze the pan. Add the remaining ingredients and simmer for 5 to 10 minutes over very low heat. Let cool, then store, covered, in the refrigerator for up to 2 months.

Prepare the Cilantro Butter: Whip the butter until creamy. Add the remaining ingredients and whip until completely combined. Refrigerate until needed.

To cook the ribs, preheat the oven to 275°F.

Place the ribs on a large cedar baking plank. Cover completely with foil so that no steam will escape. Place in the oven and cook for 2½ to 3 hours, or until the meat is fork tender. Note: Juices may accumulate on the plank. To avoid spillage, you can set the plank on a rimmed cookie sheet. Remove from the oven and drain off any excess liquid.

Increase the oven temperature to 400°F.

Place the corn cob pieces on another plank and bake for 12 to 15 minutes, or until lightly browned on the edges.

Liberally baste the ribs with the BBQ sauce. Return to the oven and cook for 10 to 12 minutes, or until the ribs are well glazed. Place the ribs on plates. Add the corn to the plates and top each piece with 1 teaspoon of the cilantro butter.

Notes: The BBQ Spice Rub is one of Chef Howie's 3 Chefs in a Tub Spice Rubs and Seasoning Blends (page 25).

Baby back pork ribs are generally between 1½- and 2-pound slabs.

If making BBQ sauce is too much for you, use your favorite purchased product.

WINE:
The "life is too short" pick:
Patrick Bottex, Cerdon du Bugey, "La Cueille," France
The "just because it's inexpensive doesn't mean you're cheap" pick:
Marenco, Brachetto d'Acqui, Piedmont, Italy 2009
Alternatives: *A semi-sweet, semi-sparkling wine to balance the vibrant flavors of the rub and the BBQ sauce. Moscato d'Asti from Italy.*

PLANK-ROASTED KUROBUTA PORK TENDERLOIN WITH SPICY PEACH RELISH

SERVES 4

24 ounces pork tenderloin, cut into four 6-ounce pieces (see note)
2 tablespoons BBQ Spice Rub (page 182 or use 3 Chefs in a Tub brand, page 25)
4 fresh cilantro sprigs

SPICY PEACH RELISH

1¾ cups diced peaches (½-inch pieces)
¼ cup diced red onion (⅛-inch pieces)
½ teaspoon seeded and finely minced fresh habanero chile
1 teaspoon fresh lime juice
½ teaspoon minced fresh orange zest
2 teaspoons coarsely chopped fresh cilantro
1 teaspoon sugar
¼ teaspoon kosher salt

Note: We like Kurobuta because of the marbling, but you can use organic pork tenderloin.

Special equipment: cedar baking plank (page 25)

Season the pork with rub. Refrigerate, uncovered, for 24 hours.

Prepare the Spicy Peach Relish: Combine all the ingredients and stir until the sugar dissolves. Refrigerate for up to 2 days.

Preheat the oven to 375°F.

Place the seasoned pork on the plank and place in the oven for 8 minutes. Remove from the oven and turn the meat over. Raise the oven temperature to 400°F. Return the plank to the oven for 15 to 18 minutes, or until the pork is nicely browned and the internal temperature is 130-140°F. Remove from the oven and let it rest for 2 to 3 minutes.

Slice the pork and arrange on 4 plates with the slices slightly overlapping. Top with the peach relish. Garnish with the cilantro sprigs.

WINE:
The "life is too short" pick:
Gangloff, Condrieu, Rhône, France 2007
The "just because it's inexpensive doesn't mean you're cheap" pick:
Mark Ryan, Viognier, Columbia Valley, Washington 2009
Alternatives: *An intense white wine with flavors of rich stone fruit and vibrant acidity to match with the peach relish. Gewürztraminer from France or California.*

KOREAN PORK KALBI
SERVES 4

20 ounces pork tenderloin, cut into ⅜-inch-
    thick round slices
1 tablespoon *each* canola and toasted sesame
    oil, blended
¼ cup Kalbi Sauce
2 tablespoons diagonally sliced green onions
1½ teaspoons sesame seeds, toasted

KALBI SAUCE
MAKES 1¾ CUPS
1 cup soy sauce
1 tablespoon minced fresh garlic
2 teaspoons finely minced fresh ginger
3 tablespoons sliced green onions
    (⅛-inch pieces)
1¼ cups sugar
¾ teaspoon coarsely ground black pepper
2 tablespoons plus 2 teaspoons sesame seeds,
    toasted
¾ teaspoon crushed red pepper flakes

KALBI MARINADE
⅞ cup Kalbi Sauce
1 tablespoon canola oil
1 tablespoon toasted sesame oil

Prepare the Kalbi Sauce: Combine all the ingredients in a bowl and whisk until the sugar is dissolved, approximately 5 to 8 minutes. Refrigerate, covered, for 24 hours to let the flavors blend.

Prepare the Kalbi Marinade: Mix all the ingredients together. Refrigerate until needed.

Prepare the pork: Place the tenderloin pieces in the marinade and marinate in the refrigerator for at least 1½ hours and no longer than 3 hours, being sure to toss them halfway through to ensure even marination.

Remove the pork from the marinade, place in a drain pan or colander, and let drain for 10 minutes.

In a large sauté pan, heat the canola-sesame oil over high heat until just smoking. Add the marinated pork and sear until browned on one side, then flip and sear for 30 seconds on the other. Add the sauce and stir until the meat is glazed. Remove from the heat.

Place the pork on a serving plate. Drizzle any remaining sauce in the pan over the pork.

Garnish with the green onions and sesame seeds.

Note: Leftover Kalbi Sauce can be strained and stored in the refrigerator, covered, for up to three weeks.

ALWAYS USE A THERMOMETER to check the internal temperature of the foods you are cooking. The following are some guidelines for interior doneness.

BEEF STEAKS	Blood Rare – 95-100°F
	Rare – 105-110°F
	Medium Rare – 115-120°F
	Medium – 125-130°F
	Medium Well – 135-145°F
	Well – 150°F+

SALMON	Medium Rare – 105-115°F
	Medium – 120-130°F
	Well – 140°F+

GAME FISH	Medium Rare – 105-115°F
	Medium – 120-125°F
	Well – 140°F+

WINE:
The "life is too short" pick:
Dr. Loosen, Riesling, Ürziger Würzgarten, Spätlese, Mosel, Germany 2008
The "just because it's inexpensive doesn't mean you're cheap" pick:
Chateau Ste. Michelle, Riesling, Columbia Valley, Washington 2009
Alternatives: *A white wine with enough residual sugar and acidity to balance the intense and exotic flavors of the Kalbi. French Chenin Blanc (Vouvray).*

ANCHO CHILI–RUBBED CHICKEN WITH ROASTED CORN AND SWEET PEPPER RELISH
SERVES 4

4 boneless, skinless chicken breasts, 6 to 7 ounces each
2 tablespoons Ancho Chili Rub (see note)
Canola oil
2 cups fresh corn kernels, blanched for 1 minute in boiling water, or thawed frozen corn
    (do not use canned)
½ cup diced red bell pepper (¼-inch pieces)
½ cup diced green bell pepper (¼-inch pieces)
½ cup diced sweet white onion (¼-inch pieces)
2 tablespoons olive oil
½ teaspoon salt
¼ teaspoon freshly ground black pepper
4 fresh cilantro sprigs
4 lime slices

ANCHO CHILI RUB
1 tablespoon dark brown sugar
1¼ teaspoons kosher salt
⅛ teaspoon chipotle chili powder
2 teaspoons smoked ancho chili powder
1 tablespoon mild chili powder blend
¼ teaspoon dry mustard
1 teaspoon paprika
1⅜ teaspoons smoked paprika

Special equipment: 2 large cedar baking planks (page 25)

Prepare the Ancho Chili Rub: Mix all the ingredients together well, then blend in a spice grinder until the salt shavings are half their original size. Store in an airtight container at room temperature.

Coat each chicken breast with 1½ teaspoons of the rub. Cover and let sit in the refrigerator for at least 15 minutes and up to 24 hours.

Preheat the oven to 400°F.

Lightly oil the interior of a cedar baking plank. Place the seasoned chicken breasts in the center of the plank.

In a bowl, combine the corn, bell peppers, onions, olive oil, salt and black pepper. Toss until well mixed. Lay the corn relish evenly over the inner surface of the second cedar plank.

Place both planks in the oven on the top or middle shelves. Roast for 10 to 12 minutes. Turn the chicken breasts over and roast for another 15 to 18 minutes, or until the internal temperature is 140°F. Remove both planks from the oven.

To serve, place the chicken on top of the corn relish on the other plank. Garnish the center of the dish with the cilantro sprigs and lime slices. Or place an equal amount of corn relish on each of 4 plates and top with a chicken breast. Garnish with the cilantro sprigs and lime slices.

Note: You can substitute one of Chef Howie's 3 Chefs in a Tub spice rubs or seasoning blends (page 25).

WINE:
The "life is too short" pick:
Dr. Loosen, Riesling, Ürziger Würzgarten, Spätlese, Mosel, Germany 2008
The "just because it's inexpensive doesn't mean you're cheap" pick:
Chateau Ste. Michelle, Riesling, Columbia Valley, Washington 2009
Alternatives: *A white wine with enough residual sugar and acidity to balance the intense and spicy flavors of the dish. French Chenin Blanc (Vouvray).*

ROASTED CHICKEN WITH HERBED CHÈVRE CHEESE
SERVES 4

4 skin-on boneless chicken breasts, 8 ounces each
12 fingerling potatoes
¼ cup olive oil
1½ teaspoons sea salt, divided
½ teaspoon freshly ground pepper, divided
1 tablespoon plus 1 teaspoon minced fresh garlic
4 cups baby spinach
6 tablespoons julienne-sliced sun-dried tomatoes in oil (¼-inch slices)
¾ cup Chablis or other dry white wine
½ cup whipping cream
¼ cup salted butter, cut into 4 pieces
¼ cup chèvre cheese
4 large fresh chervil sprigs

HERBED CHÈVRE STUFFING
6 tablespoons chèvre cheese
1 tablespoon cream cheese
1½ teaspoons minced fresh chervil
½ teaspoon minced fresh chives
½ teaspoon very finely minced fresh Italian parsley
1½ teaspoons extra-virgin olive oil

Prepare the Herbed Chèvre Stuffing: In a bowl, combine all the ingredients and mix until well blended. Chill overnight, allowing the flavors to blend.

To prepare the chicken, loosen the skin of each chicken breast. Place the stuffing under the skin and spread over the breast, keeping the skin intact. Store in the refrigerator until needed. This step can be done up to 24 hours in advance.

Cook the potatoes in boiling water to cover for 6 to 8 minutes. Let cool, then cut in half lengthwise.

Preheat the oven to 400°F.

Heat the olive oil in a large ovenproof sauté pan over medium-high heat. Season the chicken on the meat side with half of the salt and pepper. When the oil is heated, place the chicken in the pan, skin side down, and cook until the skin is golden brown. Turn the chicken over and place the potatoes around the outside edges of the pan.

Transfer the pan to the oven and roast until the internal temperature of the chicken is 130-135°F, approximately 9 to 11 minutes. Remove the chicken breasts and potatoes from the pan, set aside, and keep warm.

Place the pan over medium heat on the stovetop and toss the garlic in the pan. When the garlic begins to brown, add the spinach and sun-dried tomatoes. Toss lightly, then add the wine and stir to deglaze the pan. Cook until the liquid is reduced slightly.

Add the remaining salt and pepper and the whipping cream. Cook until reduced slightly, then remove from the heat and gradually add the butter, stirring to blend it into the sauce.

Pour the spinach mixture into the center of 4 bowls. Place the roasted potatoes on top of the spinach. Place the chicken breasts on top of the potatoes. Crumble the chèvre around the outside of the chicken. Garnish with chervil sprigs.

WINE:
The "life is too short" pick:
Didier Dagueneau, "Pur Sang," Pouilly-Fumé, Loire, France 2007
The "just because it's inexpensive doesn't mean you're cheap" pick:
Efeste, Sauvignon Blanc, "Feral," Evergreen Vineyard, Columbia Valley, Washington 2010
Alternatives: *A white wine with racy acidity and earthy notes to balance the chèvre stuffing. New Zealand Sauvignon Blanc or Spanish Verdejo.*

PEPPERED CHICKEN WITH TRUFFLE VINAIGRETTE
SERVES 4

20 ounces fingerling potatoes
    (about 30 to 32 potatoes)
24 ounces boneless, skinless chicken breasts,
    cut into eight 3-ounce, ½-inch-thick
    medallions
2 tablespoons canola oil
1½ teaspoons sea salt, divided
2 teaspoons Three-Peppercorn Dry Crust
¼ cup olive oil, divided
1½ teaspoons finely minced garlic
¼ cup thinly sliced fresh basil
16 baby yellow pear tomatoes, halved
16 Sweet 100 baby red cherry tomatoes, halved
½ cup Chicken Stock (page 120)
¾ cup Black Truffle Vinaigrette (page 63), divided
½ teaspoon pink sea salt
4 fresh basil sprigs

THREE-PEPPERCORN DRY CRUST
MAKES 2 TABLESPOONS
1 tablespoon pink peppercorns
1 tablespoon green peppercorns
1 tablespoon black peppercorns

Prepare the Three-Peppercorn Dry Crust:
Combine all the ingredients and mix well.
Place in a spice grinder and pulse until
coarsely ground. Even though you need only
2 teaspoons for this recipe, you'll have to make
the 2-tablespoon batch so it works properly
in the spice grinder. Store in an airtight
container at room temperature.

Blanch the potatoes in boiling water for
5 minutes. Cut in half lengthwise.

Brush the chicken medallions with the canola
oil. Season each piece with ⅛ teaspoon
of sea salt, then press ¼ teaspoon of the
three-peppercorn dry crust onto one side
of each medallion.

Preheat the oven to 450°F.

In a roasting pan, toss the potatoes with half
of the olive oil, the remaining sea salt, and the
garlic and sliced basil. Roast in the oven for
8 to 10 minutes, or until the potatoes are
golden brown and tender.

Place the remaining olive oil on a flat-top grill
or in a large sauté pan over medium-high heat.
Sear the chicken, peppercorn side down. When
lightly browned, turn the chicken over and
cook to an internal temperature of 130-135°F.

Remove the potatoes from the oven and divide
among 4 plates, with a concentration in the
center of the plate. Distribute the tomatoes
evenly over the plates.

Meanwhile heat the chicken stock in a small
saucepan. When the stock is boiling, remove
the pan from the heat and add ½ cup of the
truffle vinaigrette. Pour the mixture evenly
over the potatoes and tomatoes. Season the
tomatoes with the pink sea salt.

Place the chicken, slightly overlapping, in the
center of the plates on top of the potatoes
and tomatoes. Drizzle the remaining truffle
vinaigrette over and around the chicken.
Garnish with the basil sprigs.

WINE:
The "life is too short" pick:
J. F. Coche-Dury, Meursault, Burgundy,
   France 2007
The "just because it's inexpensive doesn't
mean you're cheap" pick:
Joseph Drouhin, Bourgogne, France 2007
Alternatives: *A rich white wine with opulent
   baked red apple and earthy-
   toasty notes. A rich Chardonnay.*

Talking about the middle of the economic crisis in 2009:

John had a big manager meeting in the back and he started crying. At first I lost it; it was the first time I had seen a sign of weakness. He was scared, so I gave him a hug and he hugged me back. I thought, jeez, I just hugged John Howie, and he showed that side of himself, that side he doesn't usually show. He does have a heart, and he was afraid for the restaurant but really more for all the people and what they were going to do. He didn't want to lose anyone. He told us to hold on, we are going to get through this — and we did. Tonight we have 235 people coming to dinner. Hold on! You just have to believe you will get through it.

KAREY COBLE
MANAGER / PARTNER
SEASTAR RESTAURANT & RAW BAR

He has always said bring me anything. It can be intimidating. He's not going to say he loves it. Normally you bring him something and he will tell you it needs this or that, but not in a rude way. Seeing him dissect something will help you learn, and you really get it — I should have thought of that, it needed a little extra green or something red on the plate, maybe some acid, a squirt of lime. This is where the learning really comes in. Much of it you do learn in culinary school, but he is so passionate about it that you learn by example.

Every guest every time. If you don't think like that, it's so easy to get into a routine. All the little touches make a difference. I see things differently now — I want to find things before John does, not just to make the boss happy, but because he has taught me how important it is. He doesn't skimp on anything, and he doesn't want us to.

JOE HAYNES
CHEF / PARTNER
SEASTAR RESTAURANT & RAW BAR

SWEETS

PINEAPPLE UPSIDE-DOWN CHEESECAKES
SERVES 4

8 tablespoons (½ cup) graham cracker crumbs

2 tablespoons salted butter, melted

½ cup crushed or minced fresh pineapple
(or canned, drained)

1 pound cream cheese, at room temperature

10 tablespoons sugar

2 large eggs

4 fresh pineapple rings (¼ inch thick),
core removed, or drained if canned

4 maraschino cherries

PECAN-CARAMEL SAUCE

10 tablespoons Caramel Sauce (page 205)

6 tablespoons chopped pecans, toasted
(⅛- to ¼-inch pieces)

Special equipment: four 3-inch-wide by
2-inch-deep springform pans or false-bottom
tins; kitchen blowtorch

In a small bowl, combine the graham cracker crumbs and melted butter. Mix until all the butter has been absorbed and there are no dry crumbs left. Refrigerate until needed.

Chop the crushed pineapple in a food processor until it is pureed, with some small chunks.

Place the cream cheese in a mixing bowl and soften on low speed with a paddle, making sure not to overwhip.

In another bowl, mix the sugar and eggs together. Add to the cream cheese, then add the pureed pineapple, and mix well.

Preheat the oven to 250°F.

Coat the pans with cooking spray. Place 2 tablespoons of the graham cracker mixture in the bottom of each pan. Using a small flat-bottom glass, compress the crust until it is solid and approximately ¼ inch thick.

Divide the cream cheese mixture evenly among the pans, smoothing out the tops.

Bake for 30 to 40 minutes, or until the cakes appear solid, with no rippling.

Let the cakes cool at room temperature for 20 to 30 minutes. Then place in the refrigerator until completely cool, approximately 6 hours. The cakes will keep, covered, for 3 to 4 days.

Prepare the Pecan-Caramel Sauce: Mix the ingredients together. Set aside at room temperature. To serve, place the sauce in a double boiler over simmering water and heat until warm and pourable. Keep warm until needed.

To serve, remove the cakes from the pans.

Using the blowtorch, lightly sear the tops of the pineapple rings. Then place a pineapple ring on top of each cake.

Place a cheesecake in the center of each plate. Pour the pecan-caramel sauce into the center of the pineapple, letting it cascade down around the cake. Remove the stems from the cherries and place a cherry in the center of each pineapple ring.

WINE:
The "life is too short" pick:
Château Tirecul La Gravière, "Cuvée Madame," Monbazillac, France 2007
The "just because it's inexpensive doesn't mean you're cheap" pick:
Chambers, Muscat, Late Harvest, Rutherglen, Victoria, Australia 2007
Alternatives: *A sweet wine offering honey, white flowers and caramelized apples.*

LEMON POPPY SEED COOKIES

MAKES 40 COOKIES

½ pound salted butter, softened
2 cups sugar
⅜ teaspoon lemon extract
1 tablespoon plus 1 teaspoon minced fresh lemon zest
2 tablespoons plus 2 teaspoons fresh lemon juice
2 small eggs
3¼ cups all-purpose flour
⅝ teaspoon baking soda
⅝ teaspoon baking powder
2 tablespoons poppy seeds

Special equipment: parchment paper

Place the butter and sugar in a mixing bowl and mix with an electric beater until blended. Slowly add the extract, lemon zest and juice, and mix until incorporated. Add the eggs and mix until well blended.

In another bowl, mix together the flour, baking soda and baking powder. Add to the butter-sugar mixture and mix until 90 percent incorporated. Add the poppy seeds and continue to mix until well blended and doughlike. The dough should be soft and solid, not sticky.

Place the dough on a floured surface and roll into a log 1½ inches in diameter and 16 inches long. Cover with plastic wrap and freeze until needed. It will keep for up to 2 months in the freezer.

When you're ready to bake the cookies, preheat the oven to 350°F.

Remove the log from the freezer. The dough should be cut while it is chilled or frozen. Cut into diagonal slices ³⁄₁₆ inch thick by 3 inches long, then cut in half lengthwise. Place the cookies ¼ inch apart on a sheet pan covered with parchment paper. Let the cookies sit for 4 to 5 minutes to warm to 45°F.

Bake for 8 to 12 minutes, or until golden brown and slightly crisp. Remove the cookies to a cooling rack and let cool to room temperature. The cookies will keep for 4 to 5 days stored at room temperature in an airtight container with sheets of parchment paper between the layers.

WHITE CHOCOLATE IRISH CREAM TRUFFLES

YIELD: 12 TRUFFLES

¼ cup heavy cream

3 tablespoons Baileys Irish Cream liqueur

¼ teaspoon vanilla extract

2 tablespoons unsalted butter

9 ounces Callebaut white chocolate, chopped (see note)

2 ounces Callebaut white chocolate, grated into very fine shavings

YIELD: 24 TRUFFLES

½ cup heavy cream

6 tablespoons Baileys Irish Cream liqueur

½ teaspoon vanilla extract

4 tablespoons unsalted butter

18 ounces Callebaut white chocolate, chopped (see note)

4 ounces Callebaut white chocolate, grated into very fine shavings

Special equipment: 1-ounce scoop; paper candy cups

In a heavy-gauge saucepan, combine the heavy cream, Irish cream and vanilla. Bring to a boil over medium heat, then remove from the heat, cover, and let sit for 15 minutes.

Place the butter and chopped white chocolate in a stainless steel bowl.

Return the cream mixture to the heat and bring to a simmer. Then pour the mixture over the butter and chocolate. If necessary, place the bowl over gently simmering water in a double boiler to completely melt the chocolate. Let the mixture cool at room temperature for 30 minutes, stirring every 5 minutes. Place in the refrigerator and let cool for 1 hour.

Remove the chocolate mixture from the refrigerator and let it sit at room temperature for 10 minutes. Using the scoop, form the mixture into 12 or 24 equal portions. Roll them into smooth balls, then roll the balls in the grated white chocolate shavings and place in the candy cups.

Return to the refrigerator for 5 to 8 minutes, or until set.

Store in an airtight container at cool room temperature.

Note: This recipe calls for Callebaut chocolate. Different chocolates have different fat contents, which may change the recipe results. Callebaut chocolate has a 25.9 percent cacao content, so if you use a different brand, it should have a similar amount.

WINE:
The "life is too short" pick:
Barbeito, Malvasia, Madeira 1954
The "just because it's inexpensive doesn't mean you're cheap" pick:
Pedro Romero, Pedro Ximenez Sherry, Andalucia, Spain
Alternatives: *A wine that features flavors of liquid golden raisins and white flowers.*

CAPPUCCINO TRUFFLES

YIELD: 12 TRUFFLES
½ cup heavy cream
2 teaspoons instant espresso powder
2 tablespoons unsalted butter
1 teaspoon light corn syrup
8 ounces semisweet chocolate, chopped
3 ounces milk chocolate, chopped
3 tablespoons cocoa powder
3 tablespoons powdered sugar
1 tablespoon ground cinnamon

YIELD: 24 TRUFFLES
1 cup heavy cream
4 teaspoons instant espresso powder
4 tablespoons unsalted butter
2 teaspoons light corn syrup
16 ounces semisweet chocolate, chopped
6 ounces milk chocolate, chopped
6 tablespoons cocoa powder
6 tablespoons powdered sugar
2 tablespoons ground cinnamon

Special equipment: parchment paper; 1-ounce scoop; paper candy cups

Mix the cream, espresso powder, butter and corn syrup together in a saucepan. Place over medium heat and bring to a full boil. Turn off the heat.

Add the semisweet chocolate to the mixture. Gently swirl the pan. DO NOT STIR! Remove from the heat and let it rest for 5 minutes, then whisk slowly to combine.

Transfer the mixture to a small bowl and refrigerate for 20 to 30 minutes, stirring every 10 minutes, until it is fairly thick. Keep it refrigerated for another 15 minutes, stirring every 5 minutes. Then let the mixture cool until it is solid.

In the meantime, line a sheet pan with parchment paper.

Using the scoop, form 12 or 24 equal portions. Roll them into balls and place on the prepared pan.

Chill until firm, about 10 to 15 minutes.

Meanwhile, melt the milk chocolate in a double boiler over gently simmering water. After it is completely melted, place it in a bowl and let it cool slightly before continuing.

Sift the cocoa powder, powdered sugar and cinnamon together in a small bowl, mixing well.

Wash your hands thoroughly. Remove the chocolate balls from the refrigerator. Using one hand, dip each ball into the melted chocolate. Roll it around in your hand, letting the excess drip back into the bowl. Place the truffle in the cinnamon-cocoa powder mixture. With your clean hand, cover the truffle with the cinnamon-cocoa mixture.

Lift the truffle out of the powder, shake off any excess, and place on the sheet pan. Repeat with all of the remaining truffles. Chill in the refrigerator for 5 to 8 minutes, or until they are set.

Place each truffle in a candy cup and store in an airtight container at cool room temperature.

CHOCOLATE HOT CHILI TRUFFLES

YIELD: 12 TRUFFLES
½ cup heavy cream
2 tablespoons unsalted butter
1 teaspoon light corn syrup
8 ounces semisweet chocolate, chopped
⅛ teaspoon cayenne pepper
⅛ teaspoon chipotle chili powder
¼ teaspoon ancho chili powder, divided
3 ounces dark dipping chocolate

YIELD: 24 TRUFFLES
1 cup heavy cream
4 tablespoons unsalted butter
2 teaspoons light corn syrup
16 ounces semisweet chocolate, chopped
¼ teaspoon cayenne pepper
¼ teaspoon chipotle chili powder
½ teaspoon ancho chili powder, divided
6 ounces dark dipping chocolate

Special equipment: parchment paper;
1¼-ounce scoop; toothpicks; Styrofoam block
or empty egg carton; paper candy cups

Mix the cream, butter and corn syrup together
in a saucepan. Place over medium heat and
bring to a full boil. Turn off the heat.

Add the semisweet chocolate, cayenne,
chipotle powder, and half of the ancho powder
to the mixture and gently swirl the pan.
DO NOT STIR! Remove from the heat and let
it rest for 5 minutes, then whisk slowly to
combine.

Transfer the mixture to a small bowl and
refrigerate for 20 to 30 minutes, stirring every
10 minutes, until it is fairly thick. Keep it
refrigerated for another 15 minutes, stirring
every 5 minutes. Then let the mixture cool
until it is solid.

In the meantime, line a sheet pan with
parchment paper.

Using the scoop, form the mixture into 12
or 24 equal portions. Roll them into balls and
place on the prepared pan.

Chill until firm, about 10 to 15 minutes.

Meanwhile, melt the dipping chocolate in
a double boiler over gently simmering water.
After it is completely melted, remove from the
heat and let it cool slightly before continuing.

Remove the chocolate balls from the
refrigerator. Pick up each truffle with
a toothpick and dip in the melted dipping
chocolate, lightly coating it completely. Stick
the other end of the toothpick into the
Styrofoam or egg carton, with the truffle
suspended in the air.

Sprinkle an extremely light dusting of ancho
powder on each truffle.

Let the truffles cool and dry completely, then
remove from the toothpicks and place in the
candy cups.

Store in an airtight container at cool room
temperature.

DARK CHOCOLATE TRUFFLES

YIELD: 12 TRUFFLES
½ cup heavy cream
2 tablespoons unsalted butter
1 teaspoon light corn syrup
8 ounces semisweet chocolate, chopped
3 ounces dark dipping chocolate
½ teaspoon cocoa powder, in a shaker

YIELD: 24 TRUFFLES
1 cup heavy cream
4 tablespoons unsalted butter
2 teaspoons light corn syrup
16 ounces semisweet chocolate, chopped
6 ounces dark dipping chocolate
1 teaspoon cocoa powder, in a shaker

Special equipment: parchment paper;
1¼-ounce scoop; toothpicks; Styrofoam block
or an empty egg carton; paper candy cups

Mix the cream, butter and corn syrup together in a saucepan. Place over medium heat and bring to a full boil. Turn off the heat.

Add the semisweet chocolate to the mixture. Gently swirl the pan. DO NOT STIR! Remove from the heat and let it rest for 5 minutes, then whisk slowly to combine.

Transfer the mixture to a small bowl and refrigerate for 20 to 30 minutes, stirring every 10 minutes, until it is fairly thick. Keep it refrigerated for another 15 minutes, stirring every 5 minutes. Then let the mixture cool until it is solid.

In the meantime, line a sheet pan with parchment paper.

Using the scoop, form the mixture into 12 or 24 equal portions. Roll them into balls and place on the prepared pan. Chill until firm, about 10 to 15 minutes.

Meanwhile, melt the dipping chocolate in a double boiler over gently simmering water. After it is completely melted, remove from the heat and let it cool slightly before continuing.

Remove the chocolate balls from the refrigerator. Pick up each truffle with a toothpick and dip in the melted dipping chocolate, lightly coating it completely. Stick the end of the toothpick into the Styrofoam or egg carton, with the truffle suspended in the air.

Shake an extremely light dusting of cocoa powder on just the top of each truffle.

Let the truffles cool and dry completely, then remove from the toothpicks and place in the candy cups. Store in an airtight container at cool room temperature.

BANANA SPRING ROLL SUNDAE
SERVES 4

CINNAMON-ALLSPICE SUGAR
MAKES 3 TABLESPOONS

2 tablespoons plus 2 teaspoons sugar
½ teaspoon ground allspice
½ teaspoon ground cinnamon

SUGARED PINEAPPLE

½ cup fresh pineapple pieces (¼- to ½-inch pieces)
1 tablespoon plus 1 teaspoon sugar

BANANA COCONUT SPRING ROLLS

4 spring roll wrappers
4 peeled banana chunks, 4 inches each
1½ teaspoons sugar
2 tablespoons unsweetened chopped or shredded coconut
2 egg whites, lightly whipped
Canola oil, for deep-frying
1 tablespoon plus 1 teaspoon Cinnamon-Allspice Sugar

For serving:
8 scoops (3 cups) orange caramel-swirl ice cream (or vanilla)
½ cup Caramel Sauce
8 washed pineapple leaves – use only the top 4 inches, and cut in half lengthwise if very wide

Special equipment: deep fryer

Prepare the Cinnamon-Allspice Sugar: Combine all the ingredients and stir to blend. Store in an airtight container at room temperature.

Prepare the Sugared Pineapple: In a bowl, combine the pineapple and sugar, and toss lightly. Refrigerate until needed.

Prepare the Banana Coconut Spring Rolls: For each spring roll, lay a spring roll wrapper on a flat surface, with a corner pointing toward you.

Roll a banana chunk in sugar until completely coated. Shake off excess sugar and place across the wrapper near the bottom corner. Press lightly.

Place 1½ teaspoons of coconut on the banana, letting it fall on both sides of the banana in the wrapper.

Bring the bottom corner of the wrapper up over the banana, tuck it under the banana, and tighten.

Brush all surfaces (both sides) of the wrap with egg white. Bring the sides up on top of the banana and press. Brush the remaining area of the wrapper with egg white and roll up tightly. Refrigerate until needed.

Heat the oil in a deep fryer to 365°F.

Place the spring rolls in the deep fryer and cook for 2 to 3 minutes, or until golden brown. Remove from the fryer and roll in the cinnamon-allspice sugar until well coated. Shake off the excess sugar, then slice in half diagonally with a serrated knife.

For each serving, place 2 scoops of ice cream in a martini glass. Place a sliced banana spring roll on the back side of the martini glass. Drizzle the caramel sauce over the ice cream and the bottom of the spring roll. Top with the sugared pineapple. Garnish by placing 2 pineapple leaves in the back side of the glass.

CARAMEL SAUCE
MAKES 1 CUP

¾ cup granulated sugar
2 tablespoons water
¼ teaspoon kosher salt
7 tablespoons heavy cream

Combine the sugar, water and salt in a heavy-gauge saucepan. Cook over medium-high heat until the sugar is completely dissolved. Then lower the heat to medium and cook until the mixture is a very light caramel color. Be careful to not get the sugar too dark — golden brown is good; dark brown will be bitter.

When the sauce is the proper color, slowly whisk in the cream (the sauce will bubble when you do this), stirring constantly. Cook for 2 to 3 minutes.

Let cool, then set aside at room temperature until needed.

WINE:
The "life is too short" pick:
Domaine des Baumard, Quarts de Chaume, Loire Valley, France 2006
The "just because it's inexpensive doesn't mean you're cheap" pick:
Maculan, Moscato, "Dindarello," Veneto, Italy 2008
Alternatives: *A sweet wine that displays flavors of honey, white flowers and caramelized apples.*

BERRIES WITH LEMON FOAM
SERVES 4

Lemon Foam
½ cup fresh raspberries
½ cup fresh blueberries
12 Lemon Poppy Seed Cookies (page 197)
½ teaspoon powdered sugar
4 fresh mint sprigs

With a large serving spoon, place a large oval scoop of Lemon Foam on each plate. Then add the berries, cascading slightly over and in front of the foam.

Place the cookies off to the side of the foam.

Place the powdered sugar in a shaker can or small sieve and sprinkle over the berries. Garnish with mint sprigs.

WINE:
The "life is too short" pick:
Inniskillin, Riesling, Ice Wine, Niagara, Canada 2007
The "just because it's inexpensive doesn't mean you're cheap" pick:
Chateau Ste. Michelle, Riesling, Late Harvest, Columbia Valley, Washington 2007
Alternatives: *A sweet wine that manages to balance its intense sweetness with vibrant acidity.*

LEMON FOAM
SERVES 4

1 gelatin sheet (or 1 teaspoon powdered gelatin)
2 tablespoons warm water
½ cup extra-heavy whipping cream
2 large egg whites
5 tablespoons sugar, divided
5 tablespoons fresh lemon juice
2¼ teaspoons very finely minced lemon zest
2½ large egg yolks
1 tablespoon crème fraîche
¼ teaspoon lemon extract

Place the gelatin sheet in the warm water and let dissolve completely.

Whip the cream to soft peaks. Refrigerate until needed.

Place the egg whites and half of the sugar in a mixing bowl. Using the whisk attachment, whip on high speed until the egg whites have stiff peaks. Refrigerate until needed.

In the top of a double boiler, combine the lemon juice and zest, egg yolks and the remaining sugar. Whisk over gently simmering water until thick, pale and doubled in volume.

Add the dissolved gelatin and whisk until completely combined. Remove from the heat, add the crème fraîche and lemon extract, and stir to combine. Transfer to a bowl and cool in an ice bath until chilled.

Whip — but don't overwhip — the peaked egg whites and whipped cream together with the chilled lemon mixture. The mixture should be very light and airy.

Refrigerate for at least 6 hours, or until set. This will keep for up to 4 days, tightly covered, in the refrigerator.

STRAWBERRY SHORTCAKE WITH ORANGE CREAM
SERVES 4

4 Orange Shortcake Biscuits (page 210)
4 fresh mint sprigs

STRAWBERRY BLEND
3 cups stemmed and sliced strawberries (¼-inch slices)
1 tablespoon fresh lemon juice
¼ cup powdered sugar
¼ cup granulated sugar

ORANGE CREAM
1 teaspoon very finely minced fresh orange zest
2 tablespoons Grand Marnier
2 tablespoons fresh orange juice
1½ teaspoons powdered sugar
½ teaspoon vanilla extract
¾ cup heavy whipping cream

Prepare the Strawberry Blend: Place 1 cup of the strawberries, the lemon juice and the powdered sugar in a blender. Blend until pureed.

Toss together the remaining sliced strawberries and the granulated sugar. Let sit for 30 minutes, tossing occasionally until the sugar is completely dissolved. Then add the strawberry puree and toss until well coated. Refrigerate until needed.

Prepare the Orange Cream: Combine all the ingredients in a mixing bowl and whip until stiff peaks form. Refrigerate until needed.

To serve, cut the top third off each biscuit; place the bottoms in the centers of 4 bowls. Top each biscuit with ¾ cup of the strawberry blend. Let sit for 1 minute, allowing the sauce to soak into the biscuit.

Top with the orange cream. Place the biscuit top on the cream, just off center. Garnish with mint sprigs.

ORANGE SHORTCAKE BISCUITS

MAKES 6 BISCUITS

2 cups sifted flour
1 tablespoon baking powder
1 tablespoon granulated sugar
¼ teaspoon kosher salt
½ cup lard or shortening
1 large egg, beaten
⅝ cup whole milk
1 teaspoon finely minced fresh orange zest
1 tablespoon unsalted butter, melted
1 tablespoon sugar crystals

Special equipment: 3½-inch round biscuit or cookie cutter

Preheat the oven to 425°F.

Sift the dry ingredients together. Place in a mixing bowl with the dough hook attachment. Add the lard a quarter at a time, beating until completely incorporated after each addition but not overmixed. Add the egg, milk and orange zest, beating until blended. Don't overmix the biscuits or they will become too dense.

Remove the dough from the bowl and place on a flour-coated cutting board. Knead the dough lightly, then roll out into a ½-inch-thick round. Cut into 6 rounds, then brush with the melted butter and sprinkle sugar crystals evenly over the tops.

Place on a nonstick cookie sheet and bake for 10 minutes, or until the tops are light golden brown. Remove the biscuits to a rack and let cool to room temperature.

Note: Extra biscuits can be toasted for breakfast the next morning.

WINE:
The "life is too short" pick:
La Sirena, Moscato Azul, Napa Valley, California 2008
The "just because it's inexpensive doesn't mean you're cheap" pick:
Michele Chiarlo, Moscato d'Asti, Piedmont, Italy 2009
Alternatives: *A lightly sparkling, sweet wine that is not cloying.*

GINGER SNAPS
MAKES 36 COOKIES

½ cup salted butter
½ cup granulated sugar
½ cup molasses
¼ cup very finely minced peeled fresh ginger
2 tablespoons 2% milk
6 tablespoons minced candied ginger (⅛-inch pieces)
2¾ cups sifted all-purpose flour
¾ teaspoon baking soda
1½ teaspoons ground ginger
1½ teaspoons ground cinnamon
½ teaspoon ground cloves
1 cup granulated sugar, for coating

Special equipment: parchment paper or Silpat

In a saucepan, melt the butter over medium heat. Add the sugar, molasses and minced fresh ginger, and bring to a low simmer. Remove from the heat and stir in the milk. Set aside and let the ginger steep for 30 minutes.

In a bowl, combine the candied ginger, flour, baking soda and spices.

In a large mixing bowl, combine the wet and dry ingredients — by hand — until completely incorporated. Transfer to a baking pan and let cool in the refrigerator. When the dough is completely cooled, roll into a 1½-inch-diameter, 16-inch-long log. Wrap in parchment paper or plastic and freeze for at least 4 hours and up to 2 months.

Preheat the oven to 350°F.

Remove the log from the freezer and immediately cut into ⅛-inch-thick rounds. Coat each cookie with sugar, shaking off any excess.

Place the coated cookies on a parchment- or Silpat-lined sheet pan, approximately 1 inch apart. Bake for 10 to 12 minutes, or until the cookies are crisp.

Remove the cookies from the pan and let cool on a rack. Store in an airtight container at room temperature.

Note: This recipe can easily be doubled.

WHITE CHOCOLATE PUMPKIN CHEESECAKES
SERVES 4

CRANBERRY-ORANGE COMPOTE
¼ cup sugar

1 tablespoon fresh orange juice

½ cup whole fresh cranberries
    or frozen cranberries, thawed

1/16 teaspoon ground cinnamon

1/16 teaspoon ground nutmeg

1/16 teaspoon ground allspice

¼ teaspoon minced fresh orange zest

¼ cup diced fresh orange
    (⅛- to ¼-inch pieces)

SPICED GRAHAM CRACKER CRUST
6 tablespoons graham cracker crumbs

1 tablespoon plus 2½ teaspoons finely ground
    almonds

¼ teaspoon ground ginger

¼ teaspoon ground cinnamon

2 tablespoons salted butter, melted

PUMPKIN CHEESECAKE MIX
9½ ounces cream cheese, at room temperature

4 ounces white chocolate, melted

1 large egg

1 tablespoon pure maple syrup

1 tablespoon brandy

½ teaspoon ground ginger

½ teaspoon ground cinnamon

¼ teaspoon ground nutmeg

½ cup pumpkin puree

EGGNOG SAUCE
½ cup vanilla ice cream

5 large egg yolks

2 tablespoons powdered sugar

¼ cup half-and-half

½ teaspoon ground nutmeg

SOUR CREAM TOPPING
1 cup sour cream

2 tablespoons sugar

1 teaspoon pure maple syrup

1 teaspoon brandy

1 tablespoon plus 1 teaspoon chopped
    sweetened dried cranberries
    (⅛-inch pieces)

For serving:

32 orange zest slivers (2 by 1/16 inch)

4 fresh mint sprigs

Special equipment: four 4-inch cake pans with
    removable bottoms

Prepare the Cranberry-Orange Compote: Place the sugar and orange juice in a small sauté pan and bring to a boil over medium-high heat, stirring until the sugar is dissolved. Add the cranberries and spices, cover, and cook over medium heat for 2 minutes. Remove the lid, push the cranberries to the side of the pan, and cook for another 1 to 2 minutes, stirring often, to reduce the liquid.

Remove the pan from the heat and let the mixture cool. Fold in the orange zest and diced oranges, stirring gently so you will not break up the cranberries. Refrigerate until needed.

Prepare the Spiced Graham Cracker Crust: In a bowl, combine the graham cracker crumbs, almonds and spices, and stir well. Add the melted butter and mix until the butter has been absorbed and there are no dry crumbs left. Refrigerate until needed.

Prepare the Pumpkin Cheesecake Mix: Place the cream cheese in a mixing bowl and soften on low speed with a paddle, making sure not to overwhip. Stir in the melted white chocolate, and then add the egg, scraping the bowl to avoid lumps.

In another bowl, combine the maple syrup, brandy, spices and pumpkin puree, stirring until well mixed. Add to the cream cheese and mix until well blended. Refrigerate until needed.

Prepare the Eggnog Sauce: Place the ice cream in a thick-bottomed saucepan. Melt over low heat. Add all the other ingredients and mix well. Heat the sauce over medium-high heat, stirring constantly with a wire whisk until it just starts to thicken.

Remove from the heat and immediately pour into a stainless steel bowl. Place the bowl on a bed of ice and continue stirring until the sauce is cold. Refrigerate until needed.

Prepare the Sour Cream Topping: In a bowl, combine the sour cream, sugar, maple syrup and brandy. Stir until well blended. Refrigerate until needed.

To make the cheesecakes, preheat the oven to 250°F.

Place an equal amount of the graham cracker crust in the bottom of each cake pan. Using a small flat-bottom glass, compress the crust until solid and approximately ¼ inch thick. Divide the cheesecake mixture equally among the pans, smoothing out the tops until even.

Bake for 25 to 30 minutes, or until the cakes have no rippling and appear solid.

Meanwhile, add the dried cranberries to the sour cream topping and stir to blend. Set aside.

Remove the cakes from the oven and, while they are still hot, carefully spoon on the sour cream topping. Return to the oven and bake for 5 to 7 minutes, or until the topping has set — tap the pans to be sure there is no rippling in the topping.

Remove from the oven and let cool at room temperature for 30 minutes, then place in the refrigerator and cool to 45°F, approximately 2 to 3 hours.

When the cakes are completely cooled, remove from the refrigerator. Heat the entire exterior of each pan with a kitchen torch or run a knife around the edge. Push each cake out of the pan and remove the false bottom.

To serve, place the eggnog sauce on the plates, distributing evenly. Place a cake in the center of the sauce on each plate, then spoon 1½ teaspoons of compote at 12 o'clock, 3 o'clock, 6 o'clock and 9 o'clock. Place the orange zest slivers over the compote and in the sauce, and a mint sprig at about 11 o'clock.

WINE:
The "life is too short" pick:
Isole e Olena, Vin Santo, Tuscany, Italy 2001
The "just because it's inexpensive doesn't mean you're cheap" pick:
Andrew Rich, Gewürztraminer, Late Harvest, Columbia Valley, Washington 2007
Alternatives: *A sweet wine offering flavors of honey, caramelized almonds and white flowers.*

MOLTEN TURTLE CAKES
SERVES 4

6 tablespoons chopped pecans
6 ounces bittersweet chocolate, chopped into
    small chunks
5 ounces unsalted butter
5 large eggs
½ cup granulated sugar
½ teaspoon pure vanilla extract
1 tablespoon flour
6 tablespoons Caramel Sauce (page 205)
8 caramels, each cut into 8 cubes
    (64 total pieces)

VANILLA WHIPPED CREAM
¾ cup whipping cream
½ teaspoon powdered sugar
¼ teaspoon pure vanilla extract

For serving:
½ cup Caramel Sauce (page 205), placed
    in a squeeze bottle and heated in
    a warm-water bath
4 scoops dulce de leche ice cream (see note)
2 tablespoons pecan pieces, toasted

Special equipment: four 8-ounce custard cups
    or ramekins

Spray the custard cups or ramekins very lightly with cooking spray. Place 1½ tablespoons of chopped pecans in the bottom of each cup.

In a medium bowl set over gently simmering water in a double boiler, combine the chocolate and butter. Stir often until just barely melted. Remove from the heat and stir until completely melted.

In a mixer bowl, beat together the eggs, sugar, vanilla, flour and caramel sauce. Blend in the melted chocolate mixture.

Ladle 3 ounces of batter into each custard cup. Then place 16 miniature caramel cubes in the center of the batter in each cup. Cover with the remaining batter, making sure that the caramels are covered with batter.

Refrigerate, covered, until ready to bake. This can be done up to 24 hours in advance.

When you are ready to bake the cakes, preheat the convection oven to 400°F. Bake the cakes for 14 to 17 minutes, or until they have a very slightly wiggly center.

Prepare the Vanilla Whipped Cream: Place the cream, sugar and vanilla in a mixing bowl and whip on medium speed until firm but not grainy. Refrigerate until needed.

To serve, starting at the left side of each plate, squiggle caramel sauce to about mid-plate. Run a knife blade around the rim of each mold and turn the cake out onto the plate, just at the point where the caramel stops. Place an egg-shaped scoop of ice cream on the right side of the cake. Top the cake with whipped cream and sprinkle the toasted pecans on the whipped cream.

Note: If dulce de leche ice cream is not available, vanilla is a nice substitute.

WINE:
The "life is too short" pick:
Quinta do Noval, Nacional, Oporto, Portugal 1963
The "just because it's inexpensive doesn't mean you're cheap" pick:
Taylor Fladgate, LBV, Oporto, Portugal 2005
Alternatives: *A fortified wine that displays intense caramelized berry and toasted nut flavors and aromas.*

BANANAS FOSTER
SERVES 4

¼ cup (½ stick) butter
1 cup packed light brown sugar
½ teaspoon ground cinnamon
¼ cup banana liqueur
4 bananas, cut in half lengthwise, then halved
¼ cup dark rum
4 large scoops vanilla ice cream in bowls

Combine the butter, sugar and cinnamon in a flambé pan or skillet.

Place the pan over medium-high heat either on a portable burner or on top of the stove and cook, stirring, until the sugar dissolves.

Stir in the banana liqueur. Place the bananas in the pan. When the bananas are completely coated and the pan is sizzling, add the rum. If you are using an open flame, the rum will sizzle and flame high; if using an electric burner, ignite the liquor with a long candle lighter.

When the flames subside, lift the bananas out of the pan and place 4 pieces over each portion of ice cream.

Bring the sauce to a simmer, then spoon the warm sauce over the bananas and ice cream. Serve immediately.

WINE:
The "life is too short" pick:
Château d'Yquem, Sauternes, France 2000
The "just because it's inexpensive doesn't mean you're cheap" pick:
Beringer, Sauvignon Blanc/Semillon, "Nightingale," Napa Valley, California 2007
Alternatives: *A sweet wine that has intense flavors of caramel apple, white flowers and bee pollen.*

APPLE TARTES TATIN
SERVES 4

4 tablespoons unsalted butter
1½ cups packed light brown sugar
Granny Smith apples – peeled, cored, and cut
        into ¼- to ⅜-inch wedges,
        to yield 5 cups
½ teaspoon kosher salt
¼ cup Caramel Sauce (page 205)
Ground cinnamon

PASTRY CRUST
½ cup all-purpose flour
½ teaspoon granulated sugar
¼ teaspoon kosher salt
1 tablespoon plus 2 teaspoons Armour lard
2½ teaspoons unsalted butter, cut into chunks
1½ teaspoons beaten egg
1½ teaspoons iced water
¾ teaspoon cider vinegar

SOUR APPLE CHANTILLY CRÈME
2 tablespoons DeKyper Sour Apple Pucker
½ teaspoon fresh lemon juice
½ teaspoon vanilla extract
1 teaspoon powdered sugar
½ cup heavy whipping cream (36% butter fat)

Special equipment: four 8-ounce glass baking
        dishes; Silpat or parchment paper

Prepare the Pastry Crust: Mix the dry ingredients together well in a mixer with a paddle attachment. Add the lard and butter, and mix on low speed until pea-sized dough pieces form. In another bowl, beat the egg, water and vinegar. Add to the pastry mixture and mix until the liquid is incorporated. Flatten the dough, wrap, and chill for at least 2 hours, or until thoroughly chilled.

To prepare the filling, melt the butter in a large sauté pan over medium heat. Add the brown sugar and cook until completely melted. Add the apples and salt, and cook for 30 to 40 minutes, or until the syrup begins to thicken and the apples are semi-browned and very tender. Remove from the heat, let cool, and refrigerate until needed.

To bake the pastry, preheat the oven to 350°F. Divide the dough into 4 equal portions and flatten into disks 3 inches round and ⅛ inch thick. Place on a Silpat- or parchment-covered baking sheet and bake for 7 minutes. Remove from the oven, turn the disks over, and bake for approximately 3 to 4 minutes, or until completely golden brown. Let cool and keep at room temperature until needed.

Prepare the Sour Apple Chantilly Crème: Mix the apple pucker and lemon juice together.

In a chilled mixing bowl, combine the vanilla, sugar and cream. Start to whip. Add the apple pucker/lemon juice to the cream. Whip until stiff peaks form. Refrigerate until needed.

To assemble the tarts, preheat the oven to 400°F.

Coat the interior of the glass baking dishes with cooking spray. Pack them full of the apple filling. Bake for 8 minutes. After the filling has baked for 7 minutes, place the pastry crusts in the oven and let them heat up.

Remove from the oven and place the pastry crusts on top of the apple filling. Let sit for 30 to 45 seconds.

Drizzle the caramel sauce across 4 dessert plates. Turn each tarte Tatin over in the center of a plate. Remove the baking dish. Just before serving, top with the Chantilly Crème and a light sprinkle of cinnamon.

WINE:
The "life is too short" pick:
Château de Cosse, Sauternes, France 2007
The "just because it's inexpensive doesn't mean you're cheap" pick:
Owen Roe, Semillon, Late Harvest, "The Parting Glass," Yakima Valley, Washington 2007
Alternatives: *A sweet wine that offers flavors of concentrated baked apples and honey with toasted nuts.*

GIVING THANKS

There are so many people to thank for this book being published. I will start with God. I'm a Christian man who aims to please God. And God has blessed me with many things, from a brain that understands both the creative and business side of this crazy profession, to a love for family, friends and community, to a passion and palate for great food. Thank you, Lord!

Next is my wife, Debra Carol Howie, the love of my life. Her incredible patience, understanding and love keep me grounded and motivated. She has taught me to think before I speak, although I still need a refresher course now and then. She lifts my spirits when I'm down, charges my battery when I'm weak, and is the most amazing wife, mother and grandmother a man could ask for.

Being the wife of a chef/restaurateur is not easy. We keep weird hours, work all days, bring home the stresses of the business, and often are not around for the support she might need. You have handled our life together and our relationship with grace, integrity and love; I couldn't ask for more. Thank you for choosing to be my wife, standing by me all these years, and supporting my every business decision, the good and the bad. I love you and look forward to the rest of our life together.

To my restaurant partners — and there are many — I want to thank and recognize all of you. From my operational partners, who are with me in the battles day in and day out, to the financial partners, without whom this and many other dreams would have never come through — you are all integral pieces of our success.

Many of you have worked with me for years, some for over twenty years. You are my rocks, the foundation on which our company is built, from the kitchen to the front of the house, from chefs and sous-chefs, to cooks and dishwashers, to managers, servers and bartenders. I appreciate all of you, and we would not be where we are today without you.

To my financial partners — you have been the best. Your patience and consistent confidence in me and our restaurants have been very helpful. From the unflappable support to the sage advice, you have all been more than I ever expected. Working with private investors has been a blessing. Your advice, investments and contributions will always be greatly appreciated.

All of my partners in my restaurants have given more than I could ever ask. Each and every one of them has sacrificed for their individual restaurants and the restaurant group as a whole. Your dedication and hard work amaze me. You are appreciated, and I'm grateful to count each and every one of you not only as partners, but also as friends and family.

Thank you for continuing on this incredible journey. You're the best!

INDEX